My focus, gc   w
people that anything is possible. I want to give back and show support
to the patients who have suffered from traumatic brain injuries and
also to their families. I want to show everyone that you can surmount
your odds and that you should never lose faith. Rhode Island State
Trooper, Brendan Doyle, gave me hope, he invigorated me, and I was
overcome by a feeling of belief. I want to continue to circulate this
motivation to any and everyone feasible. My desire is to give people a
substantial drive internally. I want to give patients a "Brendan Doyle"
of their own. I would like to be a person that others can look up to for
hope, for inspiration, and to re-energize their beliefs if they start to
think otherwise.

I don't want people to feel bad for me and I don't want people
to feel bad for themselves. Instead, I hope they learn from my story
and are able to take bits and pieces of each person's state of affairs I
mention on perseverance. It's a prize within itself, turning the most
tragic situations into just a bump in the road. I'm honored to share my
successful story and I can only wish to positively affect other families
and patients effort when times are rough.

"*A*s one person I cannot change the world,
but I can change the world of one person."

~Paul Shane Spear

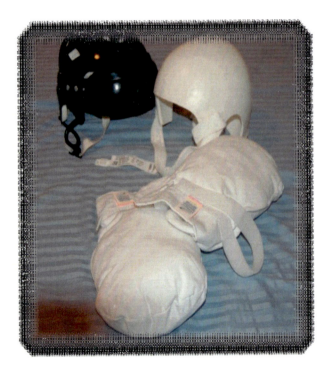

> *"How vain it is*
> *to sit down and write*
> *when you have not stood up to live"*
> *~Henry David Thoreau*

     My odds of surviving through the night of June 19, 2010 were fifteen percent at best, and my likelihood of living was minimal. You could slice that probability down to five percent at best for me to ever see a normal, healthy lifestyle again. If I were able to pull through, it would be very rare to see me manage and function under my own power; it was negligible at worst. These results seem to be somewhat metaphysical or supernatural. It isn't practical and you have to see it to believe it because it's like I hit the Powerball, and not only did I hit it once, but over and over again, because each step of the way I needed a miracle.

> *"How can you recite about life when*
> *you have nothing to share, living on a prayer*
> *all the way to the sequel, from the high's to the low's,*
> *the evil to the peaceful, a wakeup call from the naive*
> *to the most intelligent people, irrelevant if you aren't*
> *willing to speak true, take a look in the mirror to see what's see*
> *through, we only live once leave your mark how you choose..."*
>
> *March 26, 2011*

     I was always happy, constantly playing sports or watching them, and I loved going to professional games. I loved New England sports teams, remaining loyal to my upbringing. I loved hanging out with my friends and meeting new people, especially girls. I could have fun doing anything and could be seen smiling at all times. I really enjoyed music, Hip-Hop and R&B mostly, I could listen to it twenty-four hours a day. I wrote my own lyrics and they usually related to my life or simply had punch lines to make you think or laugh. If you could make me laugh you were alright in my book. I always tried to keep myself busy because I didn't like sitting around, and therefore I was always on the go. I would describe myself as a very social person, which was a useful skill where I grew up.

I grew up in the town of Johnston, Rhode Island. A small place where everyone seemed to know everyone else's business and word would spread like wild fire. June 19, 2010 the town caught fire and burst into flames as the news spread quickly of the night I had just experienced. I never had an injury in my life besides a minor sprained ankle sometimes, and a jammed thumb here and there from playing basketball. All of a sudden though, I was in Rhode Island Hospital, the Neuro Intensive Care Unit (NICU), laying there on my death bed fighting for it all on life support! Completely out of the blue, it was so unexpected no one could have seen it coming in a million years. I don't think any twenty-two year old guy expects to be monitored on a minute to minute basis fighting for his life.

I had no complaints, in fact, I thought I had it easy throughout the first twenty-two years of my life, but just like that it all changed in the spur of a moment. In the blink of an eye, just like that your life can change. I learned to take nothing for granted, but it was too late and I learned it the hard way. As stubborn as I was, I always thought I was untouchable and thought, "that won't happen to me, nothing can." When you hear a story like this you think, "that can't happen to me." It can though, just like a simple car accident could happen because you can't control everything or everyone. Maybe you drive cautiously, but you can't control the other reckless drivers on the road.

"*G*rowing up we think we know it all, but to really grow,
is to gain knowledge and counter what you encounter..."

March 16, 2011

Life to me is a blessing in disguise, and you never truly know what you have until it's gone. For example who can smell? Imagine a life not being able to smell a home cooked meal, or the scent of your girlfriend, husband or wife. It just doesn't seem right does it? As soon as something is taken away from you, you appreciate what you had. You can sulk about it, but where does that get you? Nowhere! Like your running in place, it puts you worse off than where you were to start off. When you are at your weakest point is the time you want to pull yourself together and be at your strongest. Remain emotionless, stand up and fight for what you believe in. Whether it be fighting for a loved one back or for your life back, anything is possible; you just have to want it badly enough and believe that you can do it. If you think negative thoughts then the results will be negative, but the opposite will work too, so think positive.

My friend Steve told me about a Documentary called *The Secret* and I was blown away at how much it related to how I feel about life now. It stated how everything is designed by the "Laws of Attraction," or to live vigorously because if you see good things in your future you'll attract those things. "Thoughts become things," or another words, whatever you think you want to make happen you can, you should use the power of your mind and self talk with the anticipation of being successful. I learned this technique from the beginning stages of my injury and still apply it to this day.

Some people grow up knowing what they want to be their whole life, for example a teacher, firefighter, or owning a business. But there are others like me that have not a clue and just roll with the punches their entire life, until something gives them a push in the right direction, or in my case a kick in the ass. Sometimes the worst things imaginable can happen to open up your eyes and show you what you're made to do, but I think we all prefer that life doesn't have to come to that. In any case you have to take the good with the bad and remain positive, in other words: everything happens for a reason. If you believe this philosophy then you can't go wrong because all the negative circumstances are really great barriers in disguise which will make you grow as a person and make you physically and mentally stronger.

Negativity is the key to failure, when you think you can't accomplish a goal is when you won't because your conscience or that little voice in your head is telling you it's not possible. Once you let pessimism take control it's the beginning of your downfall. I had traumatic damage to the frontal lobe of my brain which controls a person's emotions. The damage done controlled me and made me more vulnerable, or in my mindset, weaker. I have to fight negative thoughts daily, hourly, and as each minute passes. I can't let them seep into my mind, harvest and grow because that's when I will begin to settle.

You always hear people complain about things that really don't seem to matter. The weather will be cold and rainy the next few days or you go out to eat and your meal tasted like crap and you wasted twenty bucks. I think people need to start thinking bigger and focusing on what really matters in life, like family and helping people who don't have as much as you or the less fortunate who were born into worse circumstances. The world doesn't revolve around you.

My family could quite possibly win a family of the year award for 2010. We are so tight knit when just a year ago I'd sleep out four or five nights a week. I would run home to shower and go to work then go out and party again and again. It was very repetitive, but it never got old. Now I depend on them for simple things such as a car ride to get a haircut or to grab me a sandwich for lunch. It's almost like I'm reliving my just turned teenage years. I finally turned sixteen got my license and I was off. I felt free and it never crossed my mind to say thank you, I never realized how good I had it. My family was always there for me and I appreciated it, but I never showed it. See, you always hurt the ones you love the most because no matter what you know they are always going to be there for you and love you.

Everyone loves my mother, Karen. She works at Johnston High School, the high school I graduated from. My father Carl is great too, he never believed in taking the easy way out, a very talented man, from being a graphic designer, to an EMT, to owning his own auto care business with his good friend Peter. They raised me to be respectful and considerate. They taught me to care for others and no matter the outcome they only care that I do my best.

My dad grew up living in a house behind my mom's and he knew her almost his entire life; I would say they raised me kind of old school. They are a perfect couple with great morals and values. They are always there to support me and are quick to tell me when I'm wrong. At the same time, they are always there to help me to fix my problems. They don't do it for me, instead, they push me in the right direction, encourage and support me. My parents are very loving, giving people who are easy to get along with.

My brother Nick is two and a half years older than I am. We weren't extra close and didn't always see eye-to-eye as we had our fair share of fights, but then again, who ever said that families are perfect? Everyone has disagreements and you're not always going to get along, but that's when you find out the true love a family or friend, boyfriend or girlfriend, husband or wife has for you. Nobody said life would be easy and what makes you stronger and closer are the hard times in life that you have to battle through. To me, family means always being there for each other and providing support no matter the task. Whether it be a parent driving his/her child to a sporting event when they're just learning how to play and cheering them on, or cooking them dinner and providing food, clothes, and unlimited love. I think you have to love your husband, wife, or children unconditionally and by any means necessary keep them safe. To me a family has a special bond no one can break. Like the saying goes, "blood is thicker than water."

Friday, June 18, 2010 was like any other day I woke up and went about my day. My parents were at work and I had the day off so I decided to go spend some money at a sporting goods store at Providence Place Mall. It was closing down and I could buy sports photographs very cheap and resell them. I was always about making a quick buck. Later that night, I decided I was going to go out with my best friend Ray Pilkington, another kid, and a girl I had asked to come.

A friend and an acquaintance are very different, which we will get to later. Before I left to head out for the night my mom, as always, yelled out, "Be careful, I love you." She was sitting on my front porch. I was being me and just rushed out the door as quickly as possible mumbling, "Yeah, yeah," in a hurry to start drinking and partying. Oh how time can change in an instant and then you wish you could take the moment back. Little did I know that could've been the last conversation I had ever had with my mother? I never hugged her, never kissed her, never said I love you back and when I think about it, it makes me sick to my stomach. I remember when I was little and always thought about time machines and being able to go back and forth through time, well this was one of those instances I dreamed of. Not to help myself, but to run back in and say, "I will mom, I love you too." It's so crazy when you look back at times and realize how small an argument is with your family or friends. We need to take advantage and cherish the times we have and enjoy them because almost no one gets a redo at life. A second chance is the greatest opportunity a man can ever be granted. All the shit you messed up and dreamed about is now a part of the major things you **will** fix and **will** accomplish, not just think about fixing or want to finish over a period of a lifetime.

The four of us decided to head down to a bar called Harborside. A few other guys I knew were at the bar, but they decided to leave because the bar closed at one o'clock in the morning instead of two. We decided we were going to meet them back downtown in Providence. We ended up at a bar, Fish Co., also known as the Fish Company, which was opened until two in the morning. It was my first time at this bar and we began celebrating the night, drinking and taking shots accompanied by jokes and laughs. A scuffle broke out a few minutes into being there, but I wasn't anywhere near the crowd, my friends and I were by the bar, it was over a drink being spilt, but it didn't have anything to do with us. From this point on though, this bigger, rowdy kid never lost focus on me for some unknown reason, until the end of the night. My group of friends carried on the night though with no worries. Toward closing time, this same group of kids were involved in another scuffle, and again, it had nothing to do with my friends or me. It resulted in them being kicked out of the club.

As time passed and the club was getting ready to close I left with the original group of three people I came with. We once again saw the bigger rowdy kid with another friend who was by the bar at the time of the scuffle, looking at us from a few feet higher on a cliff wall. Ray decided we should stay behind and he walked over to tell them we didn't want any problems. Ray had gotten along with the calmer kid on the cliff wall earlier near the bar while the others got into the confrontation. The kid who was tranquil with Ray shook hands, but all that time they spent squashing any possible problems, the "tough guy" had his eyes locked on me. Both of them shook hands with Ray, but the "tough guy" turned his back like he was going to walk away and then proceeded to turn around and sucker shot Ray. They battled and rolled around for a few minutes until Ray got the advantage and was able to get himself up. By the end of Ray's scuffle two other kids who were also part of the group in the club had made their way over and saw what had happened. All of them just ran away as Ray made his way back toward us, the only problem was he wasn't the only one blind sided. Ray screamed out my name and eventually found me. I was lying on the concrete not moving or responsive, I was unconscious.

When he had been struck I took a step in his direction to help. The girl I had taken out for the night grabbed my arm to pull me back. At the moment she tugged on me I was struck, completely blind sided to the left side of my head. I immediately dropped to the ground and smashed the right side of my head on to the concrete curb. Ray approached my body as I was laying in the girl's arms with my eyes closed, not knowing what had happened to me. He was nervous and concerned, but trying to remain as calm as possible. The Providence Police arrived a few minutes later. Ray tried to explain what he knew had happened. He pleaded with the police to get an ambulance and the two officers continued to ignore him or respond by saying, "He is drunk," and, "He just got knocked out for a little bit," as they acted the least bit concerned. In fact, they told Ray to pick me up and take me home. It would be nice if you had a little more concern and took your job more seriously instead of your ego. The two officers continued to try and question my friend Ray while he tried to point out the same two kids who had been part of the group from inside the club and had just watched their friend get into the scuffle with Ray on the cliff wall. They were now watching over me, any connection? We'll never know because I never ended up finding out who hit me, and the police never asked the two kids for information showing a real lack of effort and professionalism. I'm not saying it's easy to spot this type of injury, but if I were moved, in my neurosurgeons mind, I would've died on the spot. Ray continued to argue my case for an ambulance and the police then started to threaten to arrest him if he didn't calm down. The police report read, "Both subjects appeared intoxicated and were unable to communicate with Police or uncooperative with Police." How did they know I was intoxicated or uncooperative when I was lying on the pavement unconscious? I believe that it must have been extremely challenging for Ray to be calm when your best friend is lying on the concrete for over five minutes, unresponsive, while the police aren't making any progress or make any attempt to render help. They were hearing Ray, but they were not actually listening to him. At this point, I just became another Providence Police Felony Assault statistic, Incident #19651.

The Fire Department Service Reports show that someone on a cell phone called 9-1-1, deploying a Providence Fire Rescue and oddly enough, not dispatched through the police personnel on scene. As the emergency medical technicians arrived at 2:30 a.m., I was assessed and evaluated on scene, and prepared for rapid transport to Rhode Island Hospital Emergency Dept. The EMT's quickly determined that I was in a life threatening situation. By 2:36 a.m., backboarded with a cervical collar, "unresponsive, with blood suctioned from my mouth, teeth clenched and pupils delayed," I was placed into the ambulance. Despite the presence of Providence Police standing around for over twenty minutes, these trained professionals obviously understood the severity of the injuries in the few minutes that they were on scene.

Ray found my phone in the middle of the street and got in touch with my brother, Nick, to tell him to go to Rhode Island Hospital. My brother was with a mutual friend, Aaron, at the time and wasn't sure exactly what he was running into as Ray informed him I had been sucker punched and was knocked out. Nick arrived to the hospital and found out I had a fractured nose and needed a CT Scan, after hearing that he decided it was best to call my parents.

"Put your money on me and its not gambling, I'm a champion handling any obstacle, these kids were no Floyd Mayweather because anyone can throw punches but my mind is my biggest arsenal..."

February 3, 2011

Around 3:20 a.m., my mom received the call from Nick. He told my parents to come to Rhode Island Hospital because I had a fractured nose but they were also doing a CT Scan, so he found it kind of funny. My parents being quick on the spot like usual, arrived in about fifteen minutes. They were not overly nervous yet, but still very weary because my mom is never settled until each night she knows both of her kids are home and safe in bed.

After arriving at Rhode Island Hospital, and then talking to my friend Ray, my parents began to become aware that the situation was more serious than originally reported. Ray began to tell my parents how the night unfolded and how I had hit my head on the concrete. Immediately, my parents locked eyes and thought of the situation that happened a few years back to a state trooper named Brendan Doyle.

He had been struck by another person while off duty, which caused him to fall and hit the back of his head on the concrete. At that moment, Brian, the liaison, had coincidently walked out and calmly stated that the CT Scan was finished, but I had to be intubated! My dad, like I stated before, was previously an EMT, so he lost it and reacted petrified and angry, simultaneously, he was calm enough to make it clear that he wanted to see me immediately. My mom started to hyperventilate; my brother and Ray didn't really comprehend the severity of the situation yet.

My parents and brother were escorted into a family waiting room where my mother couldn't stand on her on own two feet. Just the thought of being in a "family waiting room" they realized it wasn't a good omen. In came a young male, red headed doctor who stated to my parents and brother "Your son has sustained a serious brain injury, a subdural hematoma, and needs immediate attention to relieve the swelling and we need your consent to operate. They are in the process of opening an operating room right now and that the neurosurgeon is here." Directly after that a woman came in and apologized to my parents saying they needed to sign a bunch of paperwork. My parents heads racing, just wondering if doctors had the right patient, shocked and trying to explain you could recognize me by the tattoo I have on my left forearm. My brother had been waiting calmly all this time thinking that some punks had beer muscles and decided to hit me and run. Figuring I'd be perfectly fine and that life would go on, he was overcome with the extremity of the situation.

I had shockingly just suffered one of the most deadly head injuries possible, a subdural hematoma, or in other words, a rapid collection of blood amongst my brain, or a very solid blood clot, also compression or pressure against my brain tissue. I was in dire need of an emergency craniotomy, and the odds weren't in my favor.

A major factor though was that I didn't need a Tracheotomy, which is when the doctor has to open a direct airway by making an incision in your throat to allow the patient to breathe. Doctors were able to avoid this procedure because I was breathing on my own and that caught the pressure on my brain stem.

The doctor asked if they would like to see me for a second because that's all they had because time was vital. My brother and father set off sprinting ahead of my mother who was trying to tell her brain to tell her legs to walk. They reached the trauma unit and just like you would see on television there were bloody injured patients all around, doctors and nurses running all over the place trying to save lives like it's the end of the world, beeping and buzzing machines, and medicines and tubes throughout patients bodies supplying the extra minutes as they cling to life.

They reached my room and there I lay on the stretcher, just like all the other patients they had run passed; intubated, clinging to my life, tubes throughout my body helping me breathe. My dad and brother were on each side of the gurney and Brian the liaison was still escorting my mom. He had her by her arms making sure she wasn't going to collapse. As she made it into the room she froze with horror; a mother's look at her son lying critically injured in the emergency room. My family surrounded the bed and spoke, with fear and with hope. Several doctors, nurses and technicians scurried all around me preparing themselves for surgery. Within a minute it was time, so my parents and brother talked to me and told me, "We love you, stay strong, and we're here for you, you're not alone." My dad squeezed my hand and prayed to God. They handed my parents the bag of clothes they cut off my body and a bunch of paperwork my dad had to sign off on to begin the emergency procedure.

The next few hours to my family are a blur. My brother went to get my car, my mom dealt with the liaison, and my dad moved their car from the front of the ER and made his way back to my mom. My parents were escorted through a maze of hallways and met with Brian, the liaison, who calmly explained the process of the procedure. He told them it would take an hour and a half to three hours to complete if successful, and explained once it was over the neurosurgeon would come through a specific door, as he pointed in the direction of where it was. He also showed them a phone, anytime they felt necessary to call, it was a direct line to the operating room and they could have an update on my condition. It was about 5:00 a.m. when the procedure began. My mom was fidgeting all over the place searching for cell phone reception. She didn't know how to remain calm and started to text some of my family members and her closest friends to call her when they woke up.

All alone, in an empty, cold waiting room, my parents huddled together praying, sitting, standing, staring out the window, wondering, and hoping, aware of the worst but almost begging for the best. Around 6:30 a.m. the morning shift began to arrive for work. Somewhere in this shuffle, my dad deep in thought, must have missed the neurosurgeon exiting the door they were told about earlier. This tiny little miracle, a petite German woman, appeared as my dad thought she might have been a cleaning lady. She was simply dressed in jeans and a t-shirt because she was on call and came rushing in from her home. My dad called my mom over and the doctor introduced herself as Dr. Petra Klinge, and she told them that the surgery was over, and that they were closing me up. With a grim, firm look on her face she began to explain that I had a very severe bleed, bruising, and swelling on my brain. She told my parents how the surgery went well but, due to the trauma my brain received they had to remove the right side of my skull. They drained the blood and stopped the bleeding but, my brain also sustained some bruising and swelling and that I was in critical condition and it didn't look good. With each "but" in her statements my parents gasped for air not knowing what was coming next.

My mom had to walk away crying and screaming, "No! No! No!" My father tried to fight away the tears and pain so that he could ask questions. He forced his mouth to move and asked, "Can my son die?" She looked him directly in the eyes and replied, "Yes." My parents were overcome into a crying state of anguish, and sorrow. Dr. Klinge continued to state that it's "minute-by-minute, he is young and strong." She informed my parents I was being placed into an induced coma. She then directed my parents to the Neuro Intensive Care Unit waiting room.

I was moved to the Neuro Intensive Care Unit (NICU), on the sixth floor, Bed 12, a large double room at the end of the unit. My parents sat in the waiting room quietly for three hours with tears in their eyes, remembering words to prayers they haven't used in years. At around 8:00 a.m. my mom's close friend Elizabeth Mantelli had also arrived at the hospital. At around 10:00 a.m., a nurse came out to get my parents and they held hands and walked arm-in-arm to see me. As they cautiously made their way into my room I was covered with bags of medication, medication to keep me in an induced coma, to fight off infections, and to ease the pain. There were tubes helping me breathe, eat, go to the bathroom, and overall, just to survive. My dad walked up to me, my mom couldn't sustain as she cried and looked from the outside. I was bandaged with half of my skull missing. My face and

head were swollen and bruised, and the right side of my hair was shaven off. My mother refused to believe it was me until my dad looked for my tattoo again with hopeful denial, only to be reassured it was me. Together, my parents met a woman named Kim, she was going to be my nurse tonight or in my parents eyes the first of many "guardian angels." She reassured my parents that I was in the best place possible, that I had one of the best (if not the best) neurosurgeons operate on me, and now I was going to continue receiving the best care. This is just the beginning of a roller coaster ride in the NICU, with family and friends standing vigil day and night.

As the hours crept by, another family, The Mercurio's, were arriving into the NICU waiting area. Michael Mercurio had been moved from Miriam Hospital to Rhode Island Hospital because they discovered he had cancer or Lymphoma on his brain. The Mercurio's immediately introduced themselves to my parents and offered them whatever they had ranging from trays of pastry, sandwiches, food, and beverages. Throughout their time at Rhode Island Hospital, my parents tried to comfort them as their family continued to pour in. They had a very large extended family and by Father's Day these two families had become one. Both families exchanged information, and both families held on to hope for both sides of the equation. It is incredible to hear this story from them because both families had never met before and were reaching out to each other for hope, comfort, and any type of normalcy still available in the world. Their family and mine are both phenomenal; the strength of the two combined was unimaginable. Each day both families went through hell, and yet they were still able to encourage each other, hoping for the best for both sides. Consistently, my family and the Mercurio's received either horrific or progressive news, and they celebrated and mourned together. Thoughts and prayers were shared for both sides of the fight.

My mom's mind continued to race as she thought of my grandfather (whom I have a great relationship). He had left ten days prior to return to his home in Florida. She pondered about how she would break the news to him without breaking him. She decided to have a friend of hers who also lives in Florida go to his house when she called to make sure he would be okay. In addition to that phone call, she somehow pulled herself together and called my work to fill them in. My mom and dad called all of my relatives, some were in Florida, some were camping with no phone service, and friends were finding out from other friends or through Facebook. My parents could not believe how quickly word was spreading and how much support there was. The intensive care unit actually had to get more chairs for all of the people coming to support my family and me. My parents said that the support was "overwhelming."

Things can go haywire quickly being in the trauma unit. A Picc Line was supposed to be inserted into the right side of my chest, but they changed their minds and decided to put in a central line. It's used to distribute medications, fluids, and test blood more efficiently as you inject into the one unit. It was another surgical procedure, and I was covered from head to toe with a white sterile sheet that had a flap open on my chest where they were operating. Everyone and everything had to be sterile because, as critical as it was to have the central line, it was extremely dangerous because it did create more possibilities for infection. My dad was asked all types of questions and, again, to sign off on tons of paperwork ranging from organ donor status to religion.

Once most of my family was gathered at the hospital, later that day they were pulled into a conference room and joined by a new doctor, Dr. Potter. Between all of my family questions were asked with great concern. Dr. Potter is a critical care neurologist and assistant professor of neurology at Brown University. He wanted to explain the procedure and describe how everything works with the brain. He drew diagrams of the brain and where my injuries were as a visual. Once again he explained and reiterated how my recovery was on a minute-by-minute basis. He also wanted to explain what complications could occur in order to prepare everyone for the worst. My parents learned that if I was to survive, some possible problems down the road were slurred speech, seizures, vertigo, difficulty in visual, balance or walking, confusion or inability to speak. They were just a few problems they would have to be concerned about. They knew I was in for a serious roller coaster ride.

Imagine being a parent and being asked, "If your twenty-two year old son codes or his heart stops, would you want him to be resuscitated?" As they stood over me, watching me sweat profusely, they prayed for any sign of hope and that I might be okay. At this point in time, I was very susceptible to pneumonia, infection and a vast number of other concerns. For days my parents lived by waiting and waiting, staying through endless hours of the night, and switching the shift over to my brother and best friend to pull the all nighters.

 Somehow my parents got an hour or so of sleep only to come running back to the hospital, in fear of what may have changed.

Sunday, June 20, 2010 was Father's Day, and I don't know how my dad managed to hold it together. It's also when a lot of friends started to hear and began showing up. A friend of mine brought in a poster board that had my nickname "Shoes" written on it (because of my last name). A nickname given to my brother and I when I was nine years old, by Vinny Jackavone our little league baseball coach. It was made with the intentions for people who visited to sign with hope.

As another day or two passed, more thoughts and prayers were shared. Food was brought from a restaurant, Luigi's, I worked at in the past. Friends cooked homemade food and cases of water and soda were stacked against the windowsill. Anything someone felt they could do to make the situation just a little more comfortable for my family, they did it.

My dad had asked if the other side of my head could be shaved because he knew that's what I would want. It made me look a little more normal even under the unusual circumstances. What a small world because the nurse that shaved my hair lived near me when I was growing up. In fact, my brother Nick played paintball with him; his name is Andrew Raspallo. By Tuesday, the only two people allowed to visit me

 in the evening hours besides my best friend, brother, or parents was my friend Paul Volpe and his girlfriend Jenna Interlini. They could visit me day or night even if my parents weren't around. Those were the only four people allowed in at any time besides my immediate family. Jenna is also a nurse so she was able to explain what was going on from time to time which made things easier for my parents.

Between Paul, Ray, and my brother Nick, there was always someone there with me throughout the night watching over me with God.

Although only certain people were allowed in at night, in the day time I had a very strong support system as well. My friends Mike Gaskin, and Kendall Saccoccio were two of my

 main supporters who were there for my parents and me almost everyday. It doesn't come as a surprise to me though, they are both very loyal.

Tuesday, June 22nd was the fourth day since I had been assaulted. It was  also the day I was fitted for the white helmet I had to wear for my own protection. That same day my parents and brother went up to my room as always, but today was one of the ups on the roller coaster ride from hell. Most of my tubes had been removed and I was only hooked up to a ventilator machine to breathe, in case of emergency, but I was breathing on my own without a struggle, and a feeding tube in my nose for nutrition. Doctors decided not to unplug the ventilator machine for another twenty-four hours because they had no idea if I'd ever be able to breathe on my own again, so it was a tremendous step.

That same day, nurses had also sat me up on the side of my bed. They asked me if I had a brother and I responded, "Yes." They asked me my brother's name and I responded, "Nick." That was considered a major step so they began to wean me in and out of the coma. Every couple of hours the nurses would turn the Propofol medication, which is a general anesthetic, off or down. It is used as a psychoactive drug to induce sleep. When it was turned off I would stretch and yawn, my arms and legs would start moving, and I became the energizer bunny. I couldn't stop moving. My parents were so excited, but the doctors who explained that the movement didn't have anything to do with the injury sustained to the right side of my brain and quickly brought them back to the reality. In my case, they didn't know if I would ever wake up, and if I woke up, if I would be able to swallow, walk, talk, think, or function. It was way too early to tell, but my family crowded around with hope and remained strong. At one point my Aunt Colleen sat close to me and counted over eighty staples in my head.

On the fifth day Ray came into my room alone and sat down with me while I was heavily medicated and unresponsive. He sat next to me and started talking to me. Praying and talking about all the good times we've had throughout the years, and wishing I would wake so we could chill. Letting Ray know that I was there with him, I had one tear as Ray watched it trickle down my cheek.

In the mean time, Michael Mercurio also continued to fight for his life and showed how much of a fighter he truly was; he went for a CT Scan and received good results. As quick as everything seemed to be turning around for the both of us though, his health took a turn for the worst. Cancer had taken over his brain and there wasn't anything doctors could do to save him. He passed away and this family that my parents had come to know and feel a part of now was gone, mourning Michael and praying for me. The Mercurio's are a strong family and as much pain as they were in, they reassured my family they would not forget about me and would continue to pray for the best. My parent's felt a void, a hole in their hearts, and once again were overcome with the burden of remaining strong with no one to relate to. Although cancer is a much different obstacle to overcome, my parents and the Mercurio's related through love for a family member and being a parent in the most tragic of situations. I was never fortunate enough to meet Michael, but he will always be remembered in the hearts of my family.

With all of the joy from my progress made, and tears over Michael's unfortunate passing, it was extremely stressful for everyone involved. It took a toll on my mom. At one point she was up then the next moment she was down. Her blood pressure was so high she had to be taken downstairs in the Rhode Island Hospital ER, even though she refused to go. They ran tests on her trying to find out what was wrong and to make sure she didn't have a stroke. My dad had to run back and forth making sure we were both okay that day. Thankfully, the next day she was better and able to cope with everything. The doctors said that her condition occurred because she was experiencing too much stress.

I started to be placed in a chair by nurses on June 24th, which was six days after the injury took place. I had to wear a helmet at all times that I wasn't laying down in bed and strapped in. I also had to wear big white gloves, almost like "Mickey Mouse" hands, to restrain myself from grabbing or scratching my head. As days passed, tubes were removed, which also removed possibile infections. CT Scans were taken every so often, at one point I had a pool of blood form that had to be watched closely because they didn't know 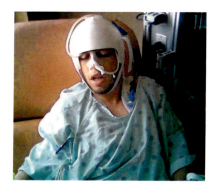 if it was a new bleed or the existing one reformed. After a few days it dissolved and that was another step climbed, and another day with no seizures.

More time passed and more days went by, and I was still unable to really speak until one day the nurses turned my medication down and I screamed out, "What the F*ck!" Nurses and my parents cheered with joy. My famous three words when most of the time a mother wishes for an "I Love You," my mother was satisfied with anything at the time. My heart rate was always monitored, but as I became a little more conscious and my medication was turned off, people would visit and my heart rate would go skyrocketing through the roof. When it came to nighttime, I was not supposed to hear anyone speak. Between my family and Ray, or Paul and Jenna, they had to be silent. Ray and my brother or Paul would sit there at night watching over me and out of sight, not making a sound because I needed to rest.

Nine days had gone by and I was still alive. The tenth day came and it was the first day I walked! I had a person on each side of me helping me down the hallway as I stumbled fast and furiously, I looked like a drunken sailor. As days went by and I continued to make progress I was given a "sitter," which is someone that watched over me to make sure I was never left alone. My catheter was removed and another step was accomplished.

On one evening, my two good friends Steve Dandurand and Aimee' Marsland came to see me and sat with me for hours. I would stretch and try to move and get free. It must have been because Steve was a close friend of  mine because I listened to him with a simple tap of the finger I would sit calmly back in the chair.  While I wouldn't listen to the nurses to calm me down until I was tied down. Everyone who visited me has a story to tell, and it's truly amazing to me when I hear because I was so heavily medicated, but still deep down knew who these people were.

On Wednesday, June 30, 2010 my status was upgraded and I was no longer considered in serious critical condition and was moved from the Neuro Intensive Care Unit to a smaller room on the 6A wing. With a graduation stroll with the help of two nurses and family, I made the walk. It was both good and bad because it showed my progression, but at the same time I wouldn't be receiving as much attention on a twenty-four hour basis. I was no longer receiving that personal one-on-one help, which made my parents extremely nervous, but they were reassured that I'd still be getting outstanding help and attention. They knew I had a long way to go.

I was settled in this new room for two days and my parents were always on top of things making sure I had the best nurses and aides, and was receiving the most attention possible, but it was not like the NICU. I began to eat and drink on my own; at one point I asked for apple sauce and was given a spoon, which I handled again on my own. My parents, with tears flowing, were ecstatic that I could do this again, conquering another unknown! When I would get upset or extremely agitated and moving recklessly my family was told the goal was to redirect my focus because suffering this traumatic brain injury was like having fifty radio stations playing in my head at once. For example, my Aunt Colleen brought me a milkshake while visiting and I had all sorts of drinks, food, and utensils on my tray alongside the milkshake. I would want to take my helmet off, so my focus needed to be redirected. Instead, the aide put the milkshake on the table and tied my hands to the chair. My parents didn't exactly like her, and I must have not liked her either because my trip to the shower one day, I grabbed the hose and sprayed her down. I never had her as one of my aides again. My mother, you could say was better at the job, knew to remove everything except for the milkshake and I was better able to concentrate and focus on picking it up and drinking it.

I became less agitated about the people surrounding me, but my worst enemy was the helmet that I had to wear. I hated it. I also hated my "Mickey Mouse" gloves, often breaking the straps that were tied to the chair and even sometimes bite them until the stuffing came out.

During the afternoon of the second day out of the NICU, the admissions representative from Spaulding Rehabilitation met with my parents and me. She talked with my parents and evaluated me for about a half an hour and decided I would be a perfect candidate for Spaulding. Spaulding Rehab is located in Boston, Massachusetts and is known as one of the best rehabilitation facilities available and one of the top ten in the country for traumatic brain injuries. This is what my parents wanted for me because it is the best.

Admissions was also was informed I needed a "sitter" while at Spaulding Rehabilitation, so they worked around it and would put me into a "net" bed, which is a hospital bed with netting around it and a zipper on the outside, for my own protection.

Thursday morning July 1st the social worker called my father and told him I was being denied for Spaulding Rehabilitation because they felt I was "walking too well." A doctor was sent in to evaluate me and didn't feel it was necessary. My parents were completely caught off guard and were enraged. My mother went back to a social worker my parents had been dealing with in the NICU and she made some phone calls to get me reaccepted. My trip ended up being delayed an extra day because of this, but I was moved on Friday July 2nd to the Spaulding Rehabilitation Center.

REHABILITATION

"Baby steps, you've got to crawl before you walk..."

June 1, 2011

I was ready to move onto the rehabilitation portion of survival and was diagnosed on a scale provided by the **Rancho Los Amigos National Rehabilitation Center**. This scale consists of eight steps used by doctors to see where a patient ranks amongst the cognitive recovery process. It's also used to explain to families or friends to make it easier to comprehend where a loved one ranks, how much help or assistance they need, or how severe their situation may be. Cognitive is a person's range of ability of thinking and memory skills. It shows judgments on reasoning and awareness, as well as decision making or problem solving after suffering a traumatic brain injury.

Rancho Los Amigos National Rehabilitation Center Scale
(Revised)

Cognitive Level I *(No Response)*
- No response to sounds, sights, touch or movement

Cognitive Level II *(Generalized Response)*
- Begins to respond to sounds, sights, touch or movement
- Responds slowly, inconsistently, or after a delay
- Responds in the same way of what is heard, seen, or felt (could include chewing, sweating, breathing faster, moaning, moving, and/or increasing blood pressure)

Cognitive Level III *(Localized Response)*
- Be awake on and off during the day
- Make more movements than before
- React more specifically to what is heard, seen, or felt
- React slowly and inconsistently
- Begin to recognize family and friends
- Begin to follow simple directions or respond to simple questions with head nods or verbal "yes" or "no" responses

Cognitive Level *IV (Confused and Agitated)*
- Very confused and frightened
- Does not understand what is felt or what's happening
- Overreactions
- Restrained in order to not harm oneself
- Not paying attention or able to concentrate for a few seconds
- Difficulty following directions

Cognitive Level V *(Confused and Inappropriate)*
- Confusion or difficulty understanding things outside of self
- Not able to complete daily activities, for example brushing teeth
- Become overloaded and restless when tired
- Try to fill in gaps of memory by making things up

Cognitive Level VI *(Confused and Appropriate)*
- Somewhat confused because memory and thinking problems (remember main points of conversation but forget or confuse details)
- Follow schedule with assistance but confused by change in routine
- Know the month and year
- Pay attention for about 30 minutes, but trouble concentrating when noisy or activity has many steps

Cognitive Level VII *(Automatic and Appropriate)*
- Follow a set schedule
- Able to do routine of self care without help
- Problems planning, starting, and following through with activities
- Not realizing how memory problems may affect future plans or goals (may expect to return to previous lifestyle)
- Think slower in stressful situations
- Able to talk about doing something, but may have trouble actually doing it

Cognitive Level VIII *(Purposeful and Appropriate)*
- Opinions should be respected, treat the person as an adult
- Be careful using slang because the person may misunderstand, also careful about teasing the individual
- Encourage use of note taking to help with remaining memory problems
- Talk with individual about their feelings

When I was cleared to leave Rhode Island Hospital and move to rehabilitation I was considered to be on step four or "confused and agitated" on the Rancho Los Amigos National Rehabilitation Center scale. Some of the things my family members were told to do to help reassure me was to tell me I was going to be okay and to take me for rides in a wheel chair to keep me moving. Also, they were told to surround me with familiar things from my life, show me pictures of family and friends, and show me items I used to use on a daily basis, for example, movies or my IPod to listen to my favorite music.

> "*I*t could be the pride in me, my spirit was broken but like a see saw through the ups and downs it could be the drive in me, because once I'm back up I'm never looking down, I got so much soul like the foot of a clown..."
> *January 7, 2011*

I was transported by ambulance from Rhode Island Hospital to Boston, Massachusetts and my mother rode with me as my dad followed. As I arrived I was taken into the main office. My parents filled out paperwork and met Dr. Bapineedu who was in charge of evaluating me with Neuropsychological examinations. I was given a bracelet and taken up to the eighth floor, room 808W or window, which overlooked the Charles River right across from the Boston Garden where the Boston Celtics play. I noticed the people all around me weren't able to function on their own as I lay in a net bed. The next day, July 3^{rd,} I was given an ankle bracelet which would sound an alarm anytime I walked through a door incase I decided to try to run away. At this time, my main goal was to escape. This bracelet would sound off even if I was with my therapists and they would have to enter a code to shut it off. On July 5th my parents came back up to Boston to visit and check up on me, even though this wasn't your average five-minute drive like those they are accustomed to in Rhode Island. They devised a plan alongside my brother and friend Ray. My parents would come on Sunday and Wednesday, while my brother and Ray would come on Saturday. Though they had a set plan in place my friend Ray would come and go ranging from two to three times a week depending on his work schedule.

Another friend of mine, Nate Hunt, worked in Boston and took the train up everyday so he was also able to come see me whether it was for five minutes or five hours it made my day. Nate was also able to communicate and relay information back to my parents to keep them updated.

Wednesday, July 7^{th,} my parents came back up for an update, a few days later on July 10th my brother and Ray came up and would get more updates, relaying everything and any sign of progress back to my parents. A day or two later Ray came back up and took me for a walk. I had to have someone with me at all times to sign me in and out, and also to put a code in to stop the alarm from ringing because of my ankle bracelet. I signed my name on my own for the first time and looked at the clock and wrote down the time too. My friend was ecstatic over these baby steps and informed my parents by text message on the spot.

Each day with or without visitors I had to follow a daily routine. I would be awakened if I wasn't already awake at around 6:30-7:30 a.m. to take my medications. I was being given all different types of medications ranging from tablets to capsules of all different milligrams. Some were used for antidepressants, others to fight off headaches, influenza, or relieve head and muscle pains. Some were used to fight seizures or used as laxatives. These medications were taken in the morning, a few times a day or just at night depending on the pill.

Acetaminophen – 325MG Tablet
Amantadine – 100MG Capsule
Butalbital (Caffeine) – One Tablet
Divalproex Sodium – 500MG Tablet
Quetiapine Fumarate – 25MG Tablet
Senna (Senokot) – Bedtime Tablet
Trazodone – 50MG Bedtime Tablet

Each day, after I took my medicine, I was brought breakfast. Not realizing that I had no sense of taste or smell, I wouldn't eat. I didn't eat for the few weeks I was there and dropped down to one hundred pounds. A nurse named Debb Fitzpatrick would speak to my parents every night before I fell asleep, she also would bring me a strawberry Hoodsy ice cream cup, and that would be all I ate all day. She would talk to me for a few minutes each night and then give my parents updates and reassure them. I was brittle, and ghostly white, you could break me like a twig. *All this time though I thought nothing was wrong with me.* I begged, bribed, and pleaded with my parents or any of my friends who came to visit to take me home. At the same time I wondered why no one would. As my day went on I would have to participate in both alone and group therapies, such as physical, occupational, and speech, which all lasted thirty minutes each. Out of twenty-four hours a day I was busy for an hour and a half. During the rest of my day I would walk the hallway lost and wondering what was going on. I would sit in bed and watch a movie or television, but at the same time stare at my clock as seconds felt like minutes, minutes felt like hours, and hours felt like days. I needed my rest, but didn't realize it and I hated my helmet and would always try to sneak it off.

When I would wake up each morning, I wasn't allowed many things and someone was always there to watch over me. By 9:00 a.m. I would take a shower as one of my aides would watch over me. I would have to sit and wear a helmet to wash up. I hated it and fought everyone there because I didn't realize these people were there to help me. I wasn't allowed to have a razor, but eventually my parents were cleared to bring me one which I used to line up my chin strap beard. Little did anyone know, my plan was to cut off my ankle bracelet, which I did one morning when I woke up early and pretended to go to the bathroom. I wanted to escape and I was determined to, the only problem was I thought I was in Florida where my grandfather lived, not Boston. My friend Ray eventually told me the story over and over again of what happened to me, but that didn't stop my focus of leaving. I was very confused and I really believed I could pull this scheme off. My plan was to sell everything my family and friends brought to me to make my way home; all my movies, my IPod, mini DVD player, toward the end my laptop, any and everything that seemed useful. There was no reasoning with me no matter what anyone would say. If I was thinking it then my mind was made up, there was no getting through to me.

As part of my physical therapy I had to walk on the treadmill and try to increase my time slowly. I began walking at a pace of 2.0 miles per hour for a few minutes without stopping. I worked my way up to 2.5 miles per hour for eight minutes. I thought that was excellent and became cocky doing the routine with my hands in my pockets telling everyone I was fine. I love basketball so they made me create goals for myself and one of my goals was to shoot hoops for ten to fifteen minutes without a break. Other things I would do was use Nintendo Wii and practice my balance or just walk on a piece of wood a few inches off the ground frontward and backward having some difficulty with that in the beginning. As time went on I followed maps and instructions of where to go in the building with help, but each time less and less help was needed and I just had people watching over me. Each time I would do these routines I thought these activities were pointless, but I'd do them to the best of my ability to show them I was fine, not realizing that's the angle they were going for.

As a part of occupational or speech therapy Spaulding planned a trip with extreme supervision to walk to CVS and the Boston Garden. I had to make a ten item list of things I was going to search for and buy on my own while they watched. We walked a little less than a mile, crossing busy streets and in the sunlight for one of the first times in months, I loved it. I would also play card games and try to learn the games or play board games and organize a schedule or goals I had for my remaining stay and my future. Nothing seemed to hit me, and each day I thought it might be the day I was going home.

Instead though, days continued to go by and as a part of group therapies I did Soduko's with between five to ten other people trying to figure the puzzles out. As a part of physical group therapies, we were given pool noodles to do basic exercises like reach up and down a few times or side to side. I got aggravated with that quickly because I felt I was ahead. Some people were older or in wheel chairs and I was clueless. I always wanted to skip out on the group sessions.

During the time I was going to therapy I would wake up and go into my closet to grab my ankle bracelet to put in my pocket because wherever I walked an alarm was supposed to sound. I stayed prepared and was waiting for the right time to make my attempt to escape. I kept thinking at night I could pull it off but my "sitter" was always ready. I began to lose hope and started to realize a little bit that I needed to listen to everyone, the doctors, my family, my friends, and therapists. I wasn't going to leave until everyone agreed I was ready, so I became more focused on proving to them, not to myself, that I was ready and it was extremely difficult.

The week of Wednesday July 14th my little cousin Anthony was going to come visit with my parents. He was so excited to see me for the first time since the NICU. My brother wasn't able to because he works for TSA at the T.F. Green Airport and he had caught an air born virus. It could never be explained, but he was taken to the emergency room covered from head to toe with a rash, which made him unable to walk, talk, or swallow. My family had it coming from all angles and this just goes to show you again how we've grown into a family with an unbreakable bond.

As time went on in Spaulding my parents were considered a "trigger" which would set my brain off to think I was able to leave. I would call them on any number I could think of. My phone was taken out of my room because of all the phone calls I was making. I wasn't even dialing the right numbers. I thought I was, but I was calling random people or places and asking for my mom and dad. I would write the numbers down on a list I created to remember them, but I would end up calling Boston Mass. General Hospital almost everyday pleading with them and screaming for them to find my parents. Eventually I was only allowed one phone call a day, and I would wake up and run down to the front desk and yell and fight with them for the right numbers. Then I'd run back to my room and scribble them down as quickly as possible waiting until I was allowed. I would call my house and leave messages, begging for answers. My parents came up the week of July 18th and were told not to come visit me until they spoke to a doctor and when they did, his advice was for them to once again redirect my focus. If I had asked to go home my parents would have to say they're there to visit only, not to take me home. Then, we would go for walks or play board games and watch some sports games on television.

More progress and more days went by, if no one was there to visit I had a special bond with an aide named Matt who took real good care of me. We watched television, he let me use a computer once in a while, he helped me when I was feeling alone and down, he always watched out for me, and he made sure if I needed anything I got it. On July 19th I had a meeting with a Neuropsychologist, Dr. Sheer, which lasted for about three hours of testing. I was nervous because I thought if I didn't do well I wouldn't leave. The testing ranged from timed categories to memory skills to writing or drawing simple day-to-day items. For example, I had to draw a clock and I drew it as a square. I ranged from average to below average, with mostly below average results in every category. It was just one month after my assault, but on July 21st Spaulding decided I was going to be able to leave July 23rd. My parents and I all met up with Dr. Sheer and discussed my results on July 21st. Dr. Carter, a psychologist, met with my family later that night and that's when I finally realized I had an injury and may not be able to do certain things for the rest of my life. I was very angry, but that same night three girls I know, Arielle Sinesi, Sami Rondeau, and Brianna Cardillo came up to visit me and helped cheer me up. We played board games and they somehow brought a smile to my face.

Friday, the 23rd came and I was cleared to be sent home. Originally, Spaulding had told my parents I would be there at least six to eight weeks and I was leaving after just three. I felt like I was back in school as a young kid. It was like I had gone through the whole day and now I was sitting at my desk waiting for the last few minutes to finish and be freed to go home. There I was sitting in my bed, watching the clock from seven in the morning until around two in the afternoon, waiting as patient as possible for my parents. I called them like I did everyday, except this time I finally called the right number on the first try and my mom answered and reassured me she would be another few minutes. I was so nervous that they had forgotten that today was the day I would be free.

Nick, my brother, came first to my room and I was so excited, but all that time I was sitting impatiently, I had never got around to packing up. With the help of my brother Nick, we packed while my parents finished up the paperwork. When we were done my parents also had made their way to my room. One of my main nurses named

Kristen had to cut off my ankle bracelet and I would be on my way. Little did she know I had already cut it off when I was busy planning my escape. She reached down to cut it and finally, I didn't have to hide it, I laughed and was on my way home with my bags in hand. I said goodbye to Larry, my roommate, who was also at Rhode Island Hospital NICU when I was, and we were off. Larry, who didn't move much, jumped up when I was halfway down the hall and wrote me a note on the back of the July calendar we had in our room which said, "Now showing today at 3p.m. Ryan's great escape, Best of Luck! I'll bed check up for you. You're a great inspiration to an old man like me, Larry." Looking back on how much we went through together daily, it almost feels like a scene from a movie.

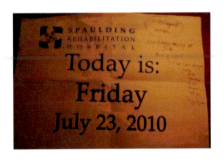

I was so excited to go home I couldn't stop smiling and crying the entire way down until we got to the entrance. We got outside and I was looking and looking for our car, but it was nowhere in sight. I asked my parents, "where's our car?" and they pointed to a white limousine. If that wasn't enough to shock me, I got into the limousine and there was my best friend Ray, and two close friends of mine Kendall and Steve. My parents had also asked a good friend of mine, Aimee' Marsland, I mentioned earlier, but she was supporting her mother on the Susan G. Komen 60-mile Breast Cancer walk. I set off on my road to recovery, but just because I was released didn't mean I was fine and my parents knew better. They were told that there were no promises and to expect the unexpected because I could react any way possible. There was no guarantee, I could come home and stare into my fridge and have no idea what to do, or how to fend for myself.

It was a huge step in the recovery process to everyone. My parents knew how long this could take, but also how fortunate I was. On the other hand, I assumed I was home and that in a few weeks or months I would be fine. I was still in denial at how serious this injury really was.

With my adrenaline pumping, I got into the limousine and I was on my way home! Earlier I was informed on how to get in and out of a vehicle because they wanted to make sure I didn't bump my head. They also informed me that I might come across some motion sickness because of all the bed rest time. Being the stubborn person I am, I shrugged it off and thought nothing of it. About ten minutes before we approached my house I started to feel sick. I remember thinking to myself are these people always right? Looking back, I'm thankful they were  always right because without their care I wouldn't be in the great condition that I'm in today. As the driver parked and we all made our way to the backyard, I didn't waste anytime and I began vomiting. My head started to feel like I was at a rock and roll concert and I was sitting on the speakers. It felt like I was being beaten senseless and I started to lose control because I didn't know if I was ready to be home. I now had no doctors or therapists and no medication for my head; I was told to take Advil. Thoughts started racing through my head and I started second guessing myself and my decision about how badly I wanted to come home. Am I ready? Can I really do this? Am I going to be alright with none of my doctors around?

I was so exhausted from just the ride home and my head was throbbing, my friends left and let me relax and get some rest. I ended up nervously falling asleep, but by the time I awoke my parents called and were prescribed what I needed for headache medication. Little did I know my parents were scared as much, if not more than I was. I was also still on certain medications like the Amantadine 100MG twice a day, Trazodone 50MG at bedtime, Butalbital (caffeine) every four hours, and Divalproex Sodium 500MG three times a day. These medications helped me with any possible migraines and were used as antidepressants or to fight off seizures and influenza.

HOME SWEET HOME

On Saturday, July 24th my grandfather flew in from Florida to surprise me. He thought he was coming to visit me at the Spaulding Rehabilitation Center. My dad picked him up from the airport while my mom and I had a meeting with Bayada Nursing downstairs to evaluate me. I walked upstairs and saw my grandfather and I was beyond shocked, I almost collapsed, I was astonished. He stayed until Wednesday July 28th with nothing but tears of joy. When I was growing up he taught me how to play checkers and we always pick up where we leave off, another game of checkers. He always has a story to tell and we spent everyday together for hours talking and playing as many games as I could handle. I'm sure he let me win the games I did because of my brain injury, but I didn't care. I was happy to spend time with him instead of just talking on the phone because the times spent with family are priceless.

> "*People* are always blaming their circumstances for what they are. I don't believe in circumstances. The people who get on in this world are the people who get up and look for the circumstances they want, and if they can't find them make them."
>
> ~George Bernard Shaw

After meeting with Bayada Nursing, my mom later found out that their speech therapist was currently on vacation for three weeks. My mom didn't want to wait three weeks without any service which they easily understood. My parents started to look into more home rehabilitation places and came upon one called the VNA or the Visiting

Nurse Association. On Thursday, July 29th a therapist named Sue came to my house for the intake visit and it was also my first day of physical therapy. Spaulding Rehabilitation recommended home rehabilitation instead of outside care because they felt it was best to wait for my bone flap, the right side of my skull, to be surgically reinserted.

As part of Spaulding's advice, I had to have support in the shower. My parents went out and found a handle bar and a special seat. My dad would help me in an out of the shower every day leaving work to come home and help me in and wait until I was done. My parents let me sleep in their comfortable temperpedic bed for months, while they slept in mine or on the couch trying to keep me more calm, comfortable and close by. When I finally felt ready to go back downstairs to my own bed they had another surprise waiting for me, a brand new temperpedic mattress to help me sleep better and a new flat screen television they had just won at a dinner raffle.

Being home, I began to fall asleep and have these feelings come over me that I had never experienced before in my life. I was waking up every night at around two or three in the morning and my head would be spinning so hard it felt like I was on a roller coaster or that amusement park ride where you spin the wheel in the tea cups so you go faster and faster. I was spinning and couldn't stop; it felt like I was going to fall out of the bed or wherever I was sitting or lying down and face plant to the ground. I never heard of vertigo before, and my dad would have to grab my shoulders to make me think I wasn't capable of falling. I was always scared because this happened almost every time I fell asleep; it made me nervous to lie down because I knew what would be coming. Sometimes it was quick, other times it would last a half hour or so, and one time my dad took the day out of work, it lasted nine hours. It was the longest nine hours of my life, spinning and vomiting every few minutes.

Monday August 2, 2010 my home rehab process began, a nurse named Judy came for speech therapy, Kim came for physical therapy, and Emily came for occupational therapy. I did one therapy at a time switching it up everyday. Everyone was blown away by the progress I continued to make. My physical therapist couldn't believe I had no walker or cane. The occupational and speech therapists were stunned that I could count change and depict what was going on in pictures or was able to tell them what the picture represented and respond quickly. I was given all types of exercises to do on my own, almost like homework. For example, sheets of paper that had questions like, "Can you name an article of clothing that begins with the letter S?" I responded with "sweater." I would have to do one or two sheets with about twenty-five questions on a page. For the physical aspect I was given a five pound weight limit and instructed to do certain exercises daily. I would perform very limited exercises with one set of fifteen to twenty repetitions. I would stand holding a chair and simply tip toe fifteen times or stand near a counter and bend my leg backwards fifteen times with five pound weights attached to my ankle.

As I moved along, Friday August 6th came, it was the same day the Beach Boys concert was playing at Foxwoods Resort Casino and I had bought my dad two tickets for Father's Day, but wasn't able to give him his gift on time. Earlier in the day I had a meeting scheduled with a woman named Robin Wyllie, the assistant director from Sargents Rehabilitation. We had our meeting and both my mom and I asked questions as she explained their program. By the end of the meeting she felt I qualified so she accepted me into the program. My mom explained how we wanted the surgery to put my bone flap back in first and then I would begin the program as soon as possible.

On Friday, August 13th I had a visit with my neurosurgeon Dr. Klinge to get an update and see if everything seemed ready for me to have my surgery. It was the first time I would meet her that I could remember. The occasion for the both of us was a milestone, very exciting and emotional. She couldn't believe I was sitting in front of her talking and functioning. She explained how my brain was at the normal point of where it was suppose to be, there was no swelling. She brought my CT Scan in and explained to me step by step how bad it really was. She told me I was ready for the surgery and I was excited. My birthday was coming up on August 22nd and I didn't care if

I had to get it on my birthday I wanted to continue to progress. Her opening was on August 25th and I jumped at the opportunity because I knew in my mind the sooner I got my bone flap put in the sooner I would begin really recovering, and not wearing a helmet. It was another step toward a more normal life again.

I continued along working with the Visiting Nurse Association on all of my therapies. I continued getting large amounts of rest and stimulated my brain any way possible by doing games like sudokos, word searches, or simply writing to myself for a few more days. By August 19th I had to go to Rhode Island Hospital for the preadmission where they did some preliminary x-rays and CT Scans to get me setup for the surgery date. A month after being home, I was discharged August 20th from the Visiting Nurse Association. Another immense mark towards my recovery.

August 22nd came, it was my birthday and I turned twenty-three! It felt amazing to just be alive; the perfect birthday present to me was coming three days later. My only wish was for the surgery to be successful. I was nervous. I tried not to show it while friends and family visited.

The next few days I kept to myself until finally the day came, August 25^{th,} my parents and I arrived at Rhode Island Hospital early in the morning about 7 a.m. I had never felt so sick in my life, so I guess it's true, be careful what you wish for because all this time I was waiting and praying for this day to come and when it was there I wanted to run. My parents, doctors and nurses tried to reassure me that I would be fine, but I was scared, numb with terror, and petrified. Calmly, the nurses came and prepared me for surgery explaining everything to my parents and me, and then my parents re-explained everything to me. Doctors came and marked my right ear with magic marker to indicate the side to be operated on, and I asked if I could keep my finger rosary on, it was given to me by my friend Ray and his parents. I had it near me everyday and wore it to any appointment or important conference as good luck and I wasn't going to stop now. All the tests ran on my bone flap came out positive so I was given back my own bone flap instead of prosthetics or artificial bone. I was given conscious sedation and brought into the operating room for a four hour surgery. A longer procedure the second time around because she had to be delicate, there was no longer any protection on my brain and she wasn't trying to save my life in a limited amount of time. She wanted to make a very fine line of stitches instead of staples so over time it would be like nothing ever happened. Eventually, after approximately five hours, with a big thumbs up, Dr. Klinge approached my parents with a shining, bright smile and told them that the surgery went perfect, and informed them there was no longer any bruising on my frontal lobe of my brain. The bleed, the bruising, and the swelling all had healed.

Once the surgery was over my parents came to visit me. I wasn't in a recovery room; I was in a regular hospital room with a tray of food in front of me. I was eating meatloaf, potatoes, and carrots. My brother also made his way up to visit and we all sat as a family enjoying the moment.

After the surgery some days went by and I had come across an ear problem that my neurosurgeon Dr. Klinge informed me it wasn't serious. Sometimes the blood dries out after this type of surgery but it goes away. I couldn't hear as well as I was used to because of this and still didn't have a great sense of taste or smell which ruined my appetite. I had two drain tubes attached to the very top of my head called Jackson-Pratt drains, located where men start to go bald first. Early in the morning, every morning, I had the blood released around five or six in the morning. It's shaped almost like a hand grenade; it creates suction and pulls or sucks the extra surgical fluids out from around the brain.

A few friends came by to visit, Ray, Paul, Jenna, and Aimee' which always made me feel better, switching the routine up each day. The comfort of having people there was always a positive. One night Jenna and Aimee' brought me a big bowl of vanilla chocolate swirl ice cream. My mom's friend Dianne came to see me and brought me a gift, it was a coin which says "Follow the footprints of the Lord it will lead you through troubled times and brighten your life." On the back of the coin it has two footprints.

My parents and I walked the halls and visited with the Neuro Intensive Care Unit nurses who worked on me and helped to save my life. I had no idea who these people were, but they had bright smiles on when they saw me. They were surprised, at the same time elated to see me. These NICU nurses had no idea what type of condition I was in since returning from Spaulding Rehabilitation, so it was nice for both sides.

On Friday August 27th my brother visited at the perfect time. I was to the point of nausea because a woman doctor was going to remove the drains that dangled a few feet from the top my head. I couldn't receive any morphine, vicodine, Advil or any type of pain medication as she began to yank out the two drains that had bulbs at the end of each. It felt like my scalp was being tugged off. I squeezed my brother's hand with both of mine with so much force I thought I was going to break his hand. She asked if I wanted to stop and I told her "No, hurry up and get this done." She then stuck four needles into the wound to numb it up and began stitching. The next day on Saturday, August 28th my parents received a phone call saying I was going to be discharged, no longer in need of a helmet because my skull was back in my head protecting my brain. Once I was granted my wish I said to my parents, "I think I'll burn that stupid helmet."

I was back home, skull back in place, and able to do more and more normal daily routines on my own. I could take a shower and I could taste a little more so I was eating more. I was going up and down stairs in my own house, and it felt good to be home living more normal. I was continuously moving forward in the right direction until Wednesday, September 1st when my dad cooked some steak on the grille. My friends Sami Rondeau and Ashley Sinesi came by to hang out. I was eating downstairs when Ashley went upstairs for some ketchup; they all heard my dish crash. As I was talking to Sami I was overtaken by a ringing noise in my head and tried to turn to her and ask for help, but a paralysis took over me and I couldn't turn my head or speak. She wasted no time and flew up the stairs to get my parents who had heard the noise and assumed the worst so they were already on their way down. I was convulsing on the futon so my dad screamed for my mom to dial 9-1-1 as he did his best to comfort me and keep

me safe. My mom dialed 9-1-1, busy at first, but when she was able to get through she informed them of my recent brain injury and that I had suffered a seizure. The ambulance hurried to pick me up and I woke up in the back of the ambulance with a rescue worker to the right of me injecting needles into my arm. My uncle, Guido, who lives just three houses down, was staring right into my eyes asking if I was okay. We took off and we were on a straightaway for the hospital. My mother rode with me, my father on his own must have taken an airplane because he was waiting for us as the ambulance backed in.

Upon arrival at RI ER, the trauma nurse could not establish an IV line in my arm, but they offered one other attempt, my neck! I refused, my arms were black, blue, purple and yellow after all the IV's and blood drawings and needles I had received throughout the entire process of the last couple of months. Never getting the needles injected on the first try there was no way I was going to have an attempt on my neck. Once moved to a Trauma Room, a nurse calmly said he could get it done on one try and he did. Another CT Scan was taken and sent to my neurosurgeon and she cleared me, she wasn't worried as she explained that the seizure suffered was very common because of the bone flap surgery I had a week earlier. After a few hours I was released and sent home.

On Friday, September 10th my stitches were removed from my surgery by a different surgeon in the office. On Monday September

13th I had an appointment scheduled with Dr. Klinge and she checked out everything with my family and I and reassured us that everything was fine.

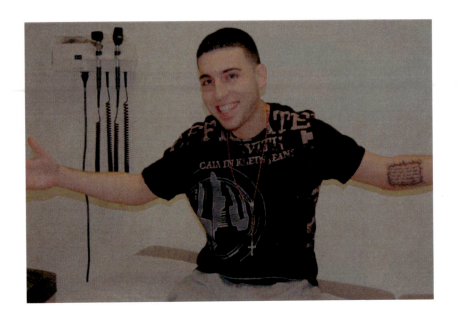

"The greatest glory in living lies not in never falling, but in rising every time we fall."

~Nelson Mandela

OUTPATIENT REHABILITATION

The next day, September 14th, after a very long night, I started Sargent Rehabilitation for the first time. My transportation was a RIDE bus, a paratransit organization provided by Rhode Island Public Transit Authority, because my parents had to work. To begin, I went on Monday, Tuesday, and Thursday from 9:00 a.m. to 2:00 p.m. in the afternoon. I was nervous and skeptical at the same time after I arrived. I was wondering why doctors, therapists, family, and friends were telling me I was doing so great and way ahead of schedule, but now I was with people who seemed like they were in so much worse condition than I was. Some suffered from extreme car accidents from drunk drivers, strokes, extreme blows to the head, some young, some older, they were in wheel chairs or unable to walk without a cane, unable to talk or communicate on their own. How was I supposed to feel normal in these conditions? However, I was suffering from what Sargent's calls "invisible deficits," or memory problems, difficulty dividing attention and concentrating on multiple aspects at one time, or the ability to learn new things and gain new insight. My five-hour days would drag along, I felt very alone and like I was wasting my time. At times I second-guessed people or their motives. I wondered am I really doing that good recovering? If so, why am I here with people who can't walk, talk, or feed themselves? It was hard to remain focused I just wanted out. It was hard to remain motivated. I would wake up and already be counting down the hours until I was getting to leave and come home.

After suffering from my seizure I needed a neurologist. My friend's mom, Jackie Pari, knew a neurologist named Dr. Andrew Blum who has a great reputation and is known for being one of the top notch professionals in this field. I went to go see Dr. Blum on September 23, 2010 for my initial appointment to talk to him about my medications. After we discussed and talked about the options for quite a while he decided to slowly decrease my medications I was on from Spaulding Rehabilitation and informed me of what medicines he would be putting me on.

I went for an appointment on October 6, 2010, to have an E.E.G, or Electroencephalography. It records brain waves or the electrical activity amongst the scalp. Electrodes are placed onto the scalp and it records for about a half an hour the flow of neurons in the brain. It is used to test epilepsy, neurological disorder, and brain death or damage after suffering from a stroke, severe migraines, or damage toward the brain.

On October 12, 2010 I went to an appointment with my primary care physician, Dr. Albert Puerini, because my ear was still bothering me. He performed an ear irrigation process on my right ear, which, combined with both suction and water, pulled out all the wax and dried blood blocking my ears after the surgery. I was having so much trouble hearing and was in massive pain laying down trying to sleep until this procedure was done. It made me feel reborn.

All this time I continued along at the Sargent Rehabilitation Center progressing and doing all the activities I thought were tedious, but doing them well. The activity intervals were split into half hour sessions I had to do each day. A half hour of physical therapy, occupational therapy, and speech therapy. Then I had a half hour on the computer, which is where I had to go onto a website called "Lumosity," and do games like timed math, create words beginning with a certain letter. Games that recorded my visual, spatial, memory, or reaction times. I walked and eventually built my way up to running on the treadmill to my favorite artist Joe Budden and listened to the same song everyday called "Aftermath" with **Rocky** interludes, keeping me focused. Each day these activities were set in a different order, eventually I had to go in and look in the set book of schedules and write it down myself upon arriving.

As a part of physical therapy I wasn't able to do a pushup when I first started. I was limited, but Lauren, my therapist, kept me motivated. We worked with a Bosu, and therapy ball. She built my strength and stamina up with squats, lunges, multiple stretches, and weighted exercises with my triceps, and biceps, shoulders, and legs. She pushed and encouraged me at all times.

During occupational therapy, Joyce, had me look at pictures and then try to rebuild the picture. I would read short paragraph problems and then try to place them in order of events. Also, I would cook with her. Once again, she was there to encourage me or show me how to complete the task for the next time. I was very frustrated in this area. It was one of my deficits I was really struggling with and would try to use different excuses never blaming myself for not answering correctly.

While in speech therapy I read articles with Jen. I also did testing packets that were multiple choice questions. We did a variety of testing, and she helped to better inform me of what I was going through.

Robin Wyllie, the Assistant Director, was also a very big part of my recovery process. Not only did she accept me into the program, but she was there to encourage me every step of the way and make sure I also felt comfortable. Anytime I was aggravated or having a rough day she was right by my side. If I just felt like talking, she found time. She would change up my schedule to keep me interested, by finding new games for me to complete. Also, she worked with me toward the end of my stay. She is very pleasant and loves her job, she never seems to be having a bad day, and would do anything for her clients.

As I finished medications and new ones were brought on by Dr. Blum; it was all trial and error to see which ones were going to work for me. He explained that each person is different and there's no guarantee which combination of seizure medication will work. I was nervous, I didn't want another seizure. I was prescribed Trileptal tablets for an overall of 1,200mg daily and Depakote extended release for an overall of 2,000mg daily. In random spurts I began to have double vision, more intense cases of vertigo, dizziness, and feeling sick to my stomach, and I just kept asking my parents if and when this would all end. I had to start getting more blood work done because they needed to test my blood levels on the medications. I ended up going to a lab where my aunt works at Urgent Care.

My mom and I were fascinated and overcome by a lady and her positivity on life, her name is Maria Barata and she works for Lifespan Lab as a phlebotomist. She's the only one who could get my

blood drawn on one attempt; we have so much in common it's scary. Dr. Klinge saved her life also; she had an enlarged tumor in her head. It was attached to her two cervical vertebrae and was cutting off her circulation in her carotid artery, so Maria lost sensation to her left hand, and her left side as her legs tingled. Battling through all odds she went into surgery on December 16, 2009. Originally, she was told it would be a three to five hour surgery, but the process ended up taking twelve hours to complete from 7:00 a.m. to 7:00 p.m. She overcame the probability of being left in a coma, crippled, or paralyzed from the neck down. She refused to be beaten and continues doing her job and working with her hands to this day! Reassuring her daughters, husband, friends, and herself everything would be alright, she never loses focus on remaining positive, enjoying every minute granted or in her words "The Journey in Life."

While I was in the Neuro Intensive Care Unit, my uncle Guido remained hopeful. We both like to gamble and he repeated over and over again I'm a fighter. "When you get better I'm taking you up to Foxwoods Resort Casino." Well that day eventually did come, and on November 7, 2010 my uncle, aunt, and I went. We gambled, we ate, we laughed, and by the time we left I had won four hundred dollars on Blackjack. I came home and my parents couldn't believe what they were seeing, as I was saying sarcastically "traumatic brain injury" with a huge smile.

Month's continued to pass by at the Sargent Rehabilitation Center and I continued to progress. All the cognitive activities the program was focusing on like improving my memory, attention, sequencing and organizing tasks, and starting and completing tasks on my own were really continuing to make strides.

My parents decided shortly after my hospital stay, that if all goes well they would like to thank everyone for their physical and emotional support. On Saturday November 20, 2010 my parents took a total of fifty people, friends and family, I invited out to eat for dinner. They took us to Wrights Farm, an all you can eat restaurant, to celebrate the progress and to thank everyone for their support. My family, friends and I ate, laughed, and took pictures, only giving me more memories I'll never forget.

A few more weeks passed and the time came where Sargent's, my family and I felt like I could begin to wean myself down because I was doing so well. I was now going Tuesdays and Thursdays from 9:00 to 12:00 p.m. Christmas came and passed and my wish or present was priceless, I just wanted to keep getting healthier. The New Year came and it was a new beginning, a rebirth, I was still trying to take it all in.

"Off the bat everyone recognizes the bad, but
I never wish on what I could've done or could've had,
I'm still eating, still breathing, leaving my
footprints in the sand all over this earth,
that's my mark disaster turns to rebirth..."

January 18, 2011

Appointments were set up after my parents kept going to the Brain Injury Association (BIA) meetings and talking to others. They heard about Dr. Frank Sparadeo. His office does neuropsychological testing, like the one I had in Spaulding Rehabilitation and an appointment was scheduled. It was a total of seven hours of testing. My first day was at the end of the year and my second and third days were on January 5th and 6th 2011. Since I left Spaulding, I had progressed greatly, leaving doctors and therapists speechless. When I was tested by Dr. Jeffrey Sheer at Spaulding I showed weakness in areas with verbal, and memory deficits. Emotionally, I tended to show signs over small situations and got agitated easily or could not fully comprehend and make something out of nothing. For example, shedding tears during a sad part in a movie or getting angry over the way something was said. Also, tests resulted in lower verbal comprehension and a low to below average visual spatial score.

This new test by Dr. Sparadeo was designed to test my cognitive status; that is my condition my brain was in after seven months of healing. In order to assess this type of testing I was brought into a room alone with only my examiner making it better for me to concentrate just like before. We did all types of testing such as visual, spatial, attention, verbal, memory, non-verbal reasoning abilities or seeing a person's reaction to something and seeing if I saw them correctly. I was also tested psychologically to make sure I wasn't suffering from anxiety or depression. This testing is designed to see where a person is struggling, but to also see their improvements as well. For example, I was given a list of words and in a timed session I had to repeat as many as I could remember. I was given the months of the year and had to say them backwards. I was also given a list of words and then given a number, for instance 240, and told to count down by intervals of three and then say as many words as I could remember from the list. I had to define words and look at pictures. Sometimes I would look at a picture and try to find what, sometimes subtle things, were missing from it. For visual and spatial I was also given a picture to look at and then had to try to reconstruct the figure in a timed setting. Overall, I was beyond nervous because I didn't think my scores would meet their standards, which would only frustrate me and, in my mind, set me back further. Every different test was timed.

Back at Sargent Rehabilitation I began to explain to them that I wanted to go back to school and they agreed and told me they thought I was ready and it would be a great idea. In Robin's words *"My success in the early tasks was key because it gave us all the belief that you could take the next step and go back to college. That opened up another whole level of cognitive retraining in a real world environment."* We looked into a Personal Health course and signed up at Rhode Island College. My dad and I met with the representative who handles the special accommodations on January 7, 2011. Special accommodations for example like having an assigned note taker, or a recorder on my desk, extra time on assignments, and/or extra exam time.

Overall, I was frustrated and didn't like the term "disabled." I wanted to prove to myself, and to everyone else who was encouraging me to take as many perks that I could get or that were necessary. I, however, wanted to do it without any help. It only added fuel to my fire, and drove me to work that much harder and only motivated me that much more. At the same time I had come to terms with my injury and tried not to be obnoxious or oblivious to the situation. All the time my therapists were trying to encourage me to take these perks I realized they weren't trying to belittle me but push me to succeed.

In this case, I learned that in going back to school after a traumatic brain injury you shouldn't be stubborn. At first you should take a little help, not because you need it, but because if you suffered such a severe trauma you may need to ease your way back into the real world, or in this instance, taking a class at college level. I decided the most intelligent and best move for me to succeed was to cover myself, and I took extra exam time just incase. When I finished my Personal Health class I ended up with a final grade of 86, or a B. I found this course very therapeutic by being out in a real world environment, and even at times, learning about my injury and the cognitive process or the six Dimensions of Wellness.

It was seven months since my injury and I went back to Dr. Blum, my neurologist, on January 19, 2011. He was impressed with my progress so we made more accommodations with my medication. I continued to take the same pills prescribed but slowly reduced the milligrams taken daily. I was on a set schedule until I got down to what I was prescribed, Trileptal tablets 900mg daily and Depakote 1,000mg extended release daily. The very next day I had an appointment with Dr. Klinge, my neurosurgeon, for a check up and she was very pleased with my results. Everyone was shocked, but happy to see me focused and progressing. I was cleared on a lot more things that I had asked questions on; such as, if I could get a tattoo on my chest or fly on airplanes; simple things in life that you wouldn't think of under normal circumstances. I was unable to be cleared to drive and I was disappointed, but she explained that because of the severity of the injury combined with a seizure she likes patients to wait a year.

We went to talk to Dr. Sparadeo on February 1, 2011 to get the results of the testing. Seven months after my assault and the testing was given again. As he began to go through the reports and explain to my parents and me, it became very emotional. He explained how he was baffled by my results after looking at the reports; he thought I was eighteen months to two years into my recovery process. You could probably see our smiles shining if you were looking down on us from the moon. Dr. Sparadeo then went into different scenarios of how people recover and he explained how left handed people recover faster than right; while I'm right handed I was recovering better than ever foreseen overall. I was performing better than predicted in a lot of categories and the ones that I wasn't were still very expected. I was struggling with problems that related to the right side of my brain, such as controlling emotions and being able to read emotional or facial expressions. Also, I was having trouble with my visual spatial abilities. At the same time, I progressed in executive functioning or the state of mental processing, language, and verbal processing. My scores were up and because certain areas were so high it showed more hope for the other areas to continue to improve.

As I continued to grow and show signs of improvement, everyone was on board to have me discharged from the Sargent Rehabilitation Center, but I had one final step. Robin Wyllie, the Assistant Director, had to go to my work with me, at B&C Liquors. As part of my future rehab, to determine if I was able to handle it. Originally thinking it would take about a month of visits I went about the first day with her and she was very pleased and couldn't believe the results as she assessed how well I remembered my job, and if I could remember how to operate the cash register. Also, she wanted to know if I could remain focused while handing back change and interacting with the customers, and if I could remember where things were located in the store. I cashiered and learned quickly on my own again. I walked around explaining the store, showing and explaining to her about how I stocked the cooler, priced the bottles, made the six packs, and how we bring things up from downstairs to restock. She was amazed by the end of the day and explained to me this was a one time visit and I could come back on my own, I was very excited.

Another major step achieved after eight months, I graduated from the Sargent Rehabilitation Center. During my stay at this rehabilitation, however, it was not easy. I had asked for meetings with the staff and my parents a few times because I thought I was ready to leave before I actually was. During each meeting the staff had explained what each area was trying to accomplish to my parents and I, and asked me to stay each time. I was very indecisive and angry each time. My parents each step of the way were always backing up the staff because of their experience in the field. After weighing my options each time I would come to the same conclusion as my parents, because I was very nervous to botch up how far I'd come in such a small amount of time. I didn't want to set myself back. At the time, I couldn't recognize my deficits anymore, they were subtle, but thankfully I didn't overreact to my feelings and listened to the staff and my parents, and also my gut notion. Before, I felt extremely uptight and anxious but would try and convince myself I was ready, this time though, I knew it was time. I really believed deep down as nervous as I was that it was time to move on and see what I was capable of. Instead of just wanting to be released, I was comfortable and I feel like a big part of being successful during this process is following the steps and gaining confidence each time a new step comes along. You have to believe in yourself, but at the same time believe in all the therapists, they know what's best for you.

I finished Sargent Rehabilitation and was now back to "working" one day a week, but not getting paid, it was considered therapy. I also had started going to physical therapy where my friend Paul worked, located a few minutes away from my house "Lepre," which is a widely known place with a great reputation. Brian, my therapist, was amazed at all of the things I was able to do so quickly. He kept reiterating how incredible it was coming back from a traumatic brain injury that within just a few weeks I was moving up in weights and continuing to be able to do different routines. I lasted there from March 3rd to May 11th and then I graduated from another therapy.

Continuing with psychotherapy I've continued to grow and make strides. With a new outlook on life I've come to realize the need and the want to focus and be "present" in life, or, in other words, to be remembered and accomplish something while I'm here instead of breezing by taking the easy way out. I've continued to try and grow and work on my deficits from my injury, like controlling my emotions and working on my visual spatial deficits with games online. Overall, I want to better myself as a man, a person, and someone to look up to after my injury.

REFLECTION

The beginning stages of my experience are remembered through the eyes and ears of my family and friends. You see this whole experience doesn't just affect me; my family and friends were and are the ones present each step of the way. I can only imagine how emotional and difficult it was to show support for me when hope was very limited. I can't imagine how much they had to endure and how much strength it took. I was the person to sustain the injury, but during all of it I was in a comatose state not hearing the possible outcomes. I was not seeing the severity of the injury or having to sit in agony as each minute passed. My parents had to be the one's to rush in and identify me while they prayed there was some kind of mistake. Once I was blind sided and my head crashed into the concrete I had no idea and no worries because I was clueless to the situation. My parents and my brother are the one's who had to sit in the waiting room with no idea what was happening, just praying. They're the ones who showed strength and battled through the moments because they had to remain strong no matter the outcome. They were told my odds were slim to none and if I did pull through that I might be in a wheel chair or not be able to fend for myself anymore, that I would never be the same. As a parent or brother how do you react to that? How do you hold it together? How are they so strong and able to keep their minds in the fight each day? Never losing faith and the desire for us to live how it once was, my strength is clearly passed down from them because I don't know how they were able to withstand these circumstances, it's remarkable.

Even as time went on during my recovery process and I moved onto different rehabilitations, it wasn't easy. My parents scheduled and then gave me rides to all my appointments. My medications had to be picked up and my parents always stayed on top of the times, double checking when to take the medications. They were on top of every move having to be made, and if I had to go through everything on my own it wouldn't have been possible because I have difficulty accomplishing the easiest of tasks in the recovery process, like just filling out certain paperwork or driving wherever.

Each different stage reached during my recuperation began to impact different perspectives. My family and friends took the responsibility of getting me through the most dangerous of times when surviving wasn't really seen as an option. As I continued to progress, they remained strong in my corner as the battle was brought face to face with me. The thoughts that run through your mind after a brain injury aren't easy to fight off. I had to find ways to remain busy, stay strong when no one came around, or push myself to continue completing all the physical and mental goals I set for myself. I have to fight off giving up or becoming lazy which would make the recovery process slow down or stop all together, and I wouldn't notice because each step of progression early on is unnoticeable, they're subtle steps. True strength and determination is shown from everyone involved and it takes everyone's focus and courage to remain positive.

"Put the pen to the pad it never works alone,
I'm so passionate you can see it in my voice
on the song, an advocate of my words the
lyrics my totem, my experiences represent who
I am when they're spoken, they'll shoot through
you like bullets because with my mouth as the trigger
I only speak the truth when I pull it..."

January 24, 2011

As I got older I had all different friends in all different clicks or groups. I was foolish to befriend a lot of these people because not everyone was there for me during my recovery process. It's fine now, but at times I needed them, it hurt and cut through me like a shark bite to a surfer, in the beginning stages, when I first came home and wasn't thinking as clearly, this really bothered me. I had visions with Ray, during my stay at Spaulding Rehabilitation, on how people were going to line up to see me and we jokingly talked about a schedule, but I knew within a month or so no one would really show that they cared because life goes on. Just like we planned in my head, I had visitors piling up to start, but as quick as they piled, they disappeared. I felt more and more alone, some was because the blow I suffered to my brain and some was just the brutal truth of life, and I learned the difference of who really cares and who doesn't. I learned the difference between a friend and an acquaintance, or what loyalty, honor and commitment to a friendship really mean to me.

"*E*veryone thinks of changing the world, but no one thinks of changing himself."

~Leo Nikolaevich Tolstoy

I've always been the type who is strongly opinionated and stubborn at the same time, but not a follower. I lead my own path and I don't believe in doing something because everyone else is. I even got a tattoo on my forearm because I feel that it describes me leading my own path. A song from one of my favorite artists, Joe Budden, says "Understand my plight, if done

right, won't seek and fail, I don't follow the path I'm creating my own to leave a trail." I hated when people would follow others because they felt weird if they didn't or thought it was the cool thing to do. Stand on your own two feet now or the longer it will take for you to become a real man. Also, I was quick to judge, but at the same time quick to trust in others. It's a weird combination I know, but I felt like I knew everything and everyone. If I wanted to do something then I was going to do it, no matter the consequence. I thought I was untouchable and just wanted to have a good time and experience as many fun, wild and crazy times as possible. I never thought or was worried something would happen to me. I would just wake up the next morning and call a friend and rant and rave about how fun the night before was. I guess you live, and you learn, and you grow.

"Being ignorant is not so much a shame, as being unwilling to learn."

~Benjamin Franklin

I was hanging out with all these different people and we were all going through the same life experiences, like high school and college. I guess I was ignorant to believe that these people were there for me as much as I was there for them. I'm a very loyal, trusting, giving, and easy to get along with person. My problem is, I believe that everyone else in the world is like I am and always sticks to their word or is there for a friend no matter what, and I mean that literally. Keep your word, and if you're doing something wrong, but you go into it knowing the consequences of your actions, then suck it up and don't bail out or don't be a rat. I guess I almost live by the perception of the Old Italian Mob movies where if you're sworn in, you're in. If you're not with me you're against me. I expected to be treated the same way, with the same respect but a lot these people opened up my eyes to the point they were extremely wide looking at the real world.

Yes, there were tons and tons of people there for me in the intensive care unit with nothing but tears in their eyes, but my fight was far from over. When I woke up and the tubes were released from my body some of the hardest times I had were after that. I wasn't thinking clearly and was alone, figuratively speaking because I always had my family and best friend behind me. If it wasn't for them I wouldn't have made it out alive or be in such a good position that I'm in today. Some people have jobs or maybe even two, some people are in school. Heck, some people have both things to worry about, but if I'm really your friend wouldn't you find time to make a phone call? To send a text message every once in a while or stop by once a month? Is it that hard to give up one Friday or Saturday night every four weeks? To me there's no excuse and I've lost a lot of respect for a lot of people. It made me realize how strong of a person I am because I had hit rock bottom and felt completely defeated, and there was almost no one to be found. Sitting home alone watching Netflix or writing to myself got old quickly. It had felt like an old western movie when the tumbleweeds go breezing by with only dessert, air, and empty space in the background. I was in a boxing match against life with my family in my corner as these fans who are supposed to be my friends were screaming for me, chanting for me like they wanted a good show. I was angry. I told myself for a while that I would never talk to these people again. However, as time went by my heart grew a little less cold and I realized they helped shape me into the strongest person I could imagine being today. You see, hard times make you into the person you become. If you've always got it easy then you're going to take the easiest path to follow. Harder times make you a man, and at twenty-two just turning twenty-three, I found myself growing into one quicker than I anticipated, but you can't always get what you want. Life won't go as planned and you have to react accordingly because there's always going to be bumps in the road. There's a big difference between a friend and an acquaintance.

Back when I was younger it was so much more clear-cut as to who was my friend and whom I just knew. When I was growing up in elementary school I would share snacks, sit next to you in class, or run around and play games with you at recess. If not, I just knew who you were and said hi and left it at that. As I got older it became a little clearer and people played sports, hung out after school, and went to birthday parties. I spent more and more time with these people and the only way to show that you're a friend is to spend time, but it's so much easier to do it at that age. As you grow older you see who's really there for you because it gets more difficult to be there because people have jobs, find more friends, or simply people change, so they have to make the decision to want to be there for you and to find time.

"I'd give you the shirt off my back in the winter time,
quicker than a sprinter's time to step up for a friend
but it takes hard times to learn a lesson, still
my swagger never left its just right, I roll
with only a few people now who are there for life..."

January 7, 2011

To me a friend is someone who is there for you through thick and thin. They remain loyal when no one else is to be found. They always stay by your side and in your corner while everyone else swaps and sways their decisions from one day to another on how they truly feel about you. A friend doesn't change up plans with you if they feel like better options come along for the night because they enjoy spending time with you. My expectations are set high for my friends because I know what I want in one and I know what I am for the people who call me their friend. I like people who are going to back me up no matter the situation. Boy or girl, courageous and honorable. All of your actions should be because that's how you are, not for pretend or to put on a show because you're in a particular situation or around certain people. I saw a quote I really like from the show *The Sopranos* and it said "No man can wear one face to himself and another to the multitude without finally getting bewildered as to which may be true." To me that means don't pretend to yourself that you're something you're not. It will always catch up to you in the end. My friends should show respect for me and accept me for me. A friend is someone who believes in me and my goals and encourages me to meet them. If I slack off they'll make me jump back on the horse and support me. Friends are always by your side even when things aren't going well because that's when you need them the most.

An acquaintance can have a positive influence on your life too. Maybe it's your boss, or someone you see once in a while, or a fellow employee. You might look up to this person but don't hang out with them often. They might be older or a friend of a friend. It's not necessarily a bad thing, but you should know how to separate the two and know the difference. It was a mistake I certainly made, everyone isn't made to become the best of friends. Sometimes I liked to hang out with certain people because they enjoyed playing basketball or gambling or going out to a party. We had similar interests, but I was quick to learn after my injury the difference between a true friend and an acquaintance. Just because you're familiar with people doesn't mean they will be there for you or show that they care for you when needed. Even the people who were there the night everything happened I barely ever hear from or have never heard from them again. I don't know how you can be so heartless or self-centered. Some people think the world revolves around them and they're in for a rude awakening when they grow up and find out the difference. In a weird way I'm fortunate this happened and showed me everyone's true colors now rather than later.

This was the biggest test of my life and so far I've passed with flying colors. No one gave me a shot or a second thought of survival from a medical standpoint. To persevere is to stand strong when there is no hope in sight but you find it in yourself anyway. I've found so much strength, courage, commitment, endurance, and the will power to live. I've never been so dedicated, persistent or patient in my life for going after success. I've never stayed so calm in the most tragic of situations. I've persevered when I felt the most discouraged and defeated humanly possible. It is an amazing feeling to overcome adversity and to go for an appointment to your neurosurgeon or neurologist or therapists and hear them all call you a miracle. You never know what you can achieve or accomplish until you put your mind to it and remain focused. It is one of the greatest feelings in the world to beat the odds and reach your goals.

"Like a young Mike Tyson I'm coming out swinging to persevere, fears stronger than love..."

March 14, 2011

Fear is stronger than love because the fear of failure was constantly playing over and over in my head even though I had the love and support of family and friends. Will I ever live a normal life and get a job and be married? Will I ever smell or taste again? Will I ever get a good night sleep again? Will the right side of my head ever be the same? Will I ever be off my medications? Will my hair ever grow back over my scar? Can I ever play basketball or other sports with friends again? I had to learn to love myself again under my new circumstances and not feel so angry at the world. I didn't feel sorry for myself, just extremely angry. I'm sure some of it was because of my injury, but most definitely some of it was because I wanted revenge. I wanted justice against whoever did this to me and I didn't care what happened to them. I wanted them to feel as much pain as I was going through, actually, I lied, I wanted to inflict more.

> "*I*'ve been screwed now I'm searching for justice
> because as a man, my word is my bond but sometimes
> even vengeance can lead you in the wrong direction
> like a compass, numbness in my mind it's not dysfunctions,
> I've proved my toughness isn't drunken, I continue to grow
> from the pain and tears like you've been chopping onions,
> I can handle any circumstance tossed in my way
> by chance, forgiveness doesn't mean you soften, I'm
> creating change like I'm morphing I'm here for a reason,
> I never take the cowards way out I stand by what I believe in..."
>
> *January 13, 2011*

Apparently time really does heal all wounds and when you have your mother and father in your ear everyday speaking rationally, you learn to move on easier. You learn to grow quicker and appreciate what you still have. I will never forget when I was first feeling really down about not smelling or tasting, my mom said to me "Would you rather not be able to see, hear or not be alive?" You see, you can always find the good in the bad, you just have to look for it. Revenge would make me feel a little better on the inside, but it will never take back what happened to me. Like I stated in the beginning, there are no time machines available. So instead I decided I'm going to learn from this and become more mature and focused on my future. I wanted to find ways to use my weakness to my advantage. I have suffered a traumatic brain injury and I'm fortunate enough to not only have survived, but to be so far ahead of schedule that it's my turn to show and give others hope. I know that I could've used it when I

was lying in a bed with netting around it, alone and lost wondering where I was and why I was there. As far as my scar goes, it builds character and I have found ways to use it to my advantage. It's my battle wound and it reminds me how far I've come in life. That and my tattoo on my chest keep me determined to never fail.

Life is a grindstone. Whether it grinds us down or polishes us up depends on us."

~Thomas L. Holdcroft

PERSEVERANCE

Beating the odds can be found in all different ways, not just in a traumatic brain injury. Being the underdog isn't easy, but everyone seems to love the story when they come out on top. Imagine growing up and being healthy your entire life and then being struck with a deadly disease, for example cancer. I know some terrific people who have been affected by this and one is a woman who I grew up with and I hung out at her house almost everyday, ate dinner there and considered it my second home. This woman is very outgoing, strong, funny, wise and free spirited. Her name is Robbin Marsland and she defeated one of the rarest forms of breast cancer.

In the years 2006 and 2007 Robbin began to experience pain and bleeding in her left nipple. Not thinking anything of it and being the strong woman she is, she continued to go about her life fighting and working through the pain. As time passed she went for an x-ray and a mammogram. The results showed no signs of anything, but the pain was too extreme to ignore as it continued to increase. She simply thought that it could've been Eczema or inflammation around her nipple. She was confused and anxious to get a cream, pill, or some type of medication to handle this itching and pain, but then received the  biggest shock of her life. She made up her mind to go see Dr. Faulkenbury, an experienced Oncologist, who decided the next step was to give Robbin a biopsy. In her own words "A picture is worth a thousand words." After this excruciating exam Robbin left and waited for her next appointment, only to find out she had a very uncommon form of cancer, Paget's disease or cancer of the nipple, for over two years at that point. She had no idea what Paget's disease was and she was short winded by all the information; it didn't seem to sink in right away.

From there she was given two options, the only choices she had, to have seventy percent of her breast removed or to have a mastectomy. Very overwhelmed, she had major decisions to make, not only about how to fight this disease, but how to break this heart wrenching news to her parents, and to her children with whom she is extremely close with. Tears poured down her parents faces, now informed of their daughter having this weight on her shoulders that she may never be able to lift, and they could not do a thing about it; Robbin held off on revealing the news to her children.

After she decided her route would be the Mastectomy, she looked into where to go after the procedure and the days couldn't go by quick enough. She met with a plastic surgeon, never once worrying about her own safety and what might happen, just concerned for her family. Finally the date arrived, she would be having her surgery September 18, 2008. Once she was informed of the date she called her son Jason and told him the news. He relayed the messaged to his sister Aimee' and she collapsed with sorrow. Her two children who I grew up with and I have never seen sad, angry, or suffering, but always happy and fun to be around now seemed to be overcome with anguish and defeat.

Just three weeks after her successful surgery Robbin was hospitalized for an infection, with intense back pains and a fever. After five days she was released, only to go another three weeks and then be re-admitted and hospitalized because of the back pains and fever once again. She was brought to the third floor, or the cancer floor, for observations. A week went by and results came in, the doctors saw that Robbin had rejected her artificial lining of her breast. Immediately, they brought her in for an operation and they removed her breast once again.

Time passed until she met with another doctor in January of 2009 who told her to wait a few months to make sure there was no infection. Her two choices now were to go without a breast or to have another surgery called the Latissimus Dorsi Myocutaneous Flap (LDMF), or to have a muscle removed from her back and dragged to her chest to be reconstructed into a breast. She was going to see her doctor every four to six weeks and they found more complications, her muscle was pulling her breast, giving her no use in her left arm to this day.

In April of 2010 she had her fourth surgery, surgeons cut and reconstructed her breast to match unsuccessfully. Robbin is such a strong woman and I am amazed by her strength and courage. Her will to fight for her life, happiness, and family is unbelievable. She has always been an amazing person since I was a child, but to know her story and know her struggles and see how she handles it all leaves me in awe. Jay has remained strong and never once showed weakness. He was there for both his mother and sister, stepping up to the challenge no questions asked. Aimee' is just like her mother, strong and fearless, she didn't falter, but instead she rose to the occasion and figured out ways to support her mother, the disease, and women as a whole. She looked into breast cancer support groups and found the Susan G. Komen 60-mile Breast Cancer walk and raised money in 2009 with a group of friends. Not stopping there, she looked further into it, as her and three friends went on their first walk in 2010 and raised $10,000. It's amazing to me to see her persevere with her family and continue her quest, now in 2011 going on her second walk with a group of six friends they raised $14,000 all going to research for breast cancer. I feel privileged to know this family and their story.

Another scenario of cancer hit your not so average Joe. His name is Joseph Acciardo. He is a great father and son. He is also known to most around the town of Johnston, Rhode Island as a teacher and football coach. He is very hard working and dedicated and expects the same out of his players. He was diagnosed with Lymphoma in 2008.

Before being diagnosed he was going through a lot in his life and it didn't hit him to enjoy the smaller things until one day after

showering he noticed a lump underneath his arm. The doctor referred to it as a pulled muscle, but Mr. Acciardo seemed to know other wise. In great shape, he knew this couldn't be. He was sent for an MRI as a precaution because his blood work looked great. The MRI results, however, showed that Lymphoma was in his lymph nodes. These nodes provide protection against harmful particles or debris before they're returned to the bloodstream. Doctors informed him that it might only be stage one which was highly curable, but still all of this information was surreal. Arriving with perfectly normal health and now leaving by motorcycle, with thoughts racing in his head faster than he was driving to get home. Everything started to go through his mind about what to expect. To him, it seemed like death was right around the corner.

He decided to try and pull himself together and do some research. He was oblivious to the situation, which most people are until they're put into one of their own to overcome. After going to see the doctor he was informed it was stage three, and after further research Joe thought it was terminal. Everything seemed to move so quick, learning on the go; he wasn't sure which direction to head. How can you remain positive when you're told you're terminally ill? How do you remain positive when you're told hope is tough to come by? Joe, however, stayed strong with his son in the back of his mind and continued to brush it off as much as possible to others. He didn't want to worry his parents, family, friends, and especially his five year old son. Courageously heading to the doctors he was informed the Lymphoma spread throughout his shoulder, chest, stomach, and spleen.

Word was also beginning to spread, and as a football coach he had a meeting with his team. More families and friends began to hear. His phone became overloaded with messages wishing him well, old and new friends began to come by his house and provide support with whatever they thought necessary from cooking to cleaning every night. The struggle began and Joe started his fight toward recovery and his second chance at life. He woke up one night and saw clumps of hair falling out of his head because he started Chemotherapy. Becoming more religious he prayed and remained hopeful and became one of the strongest people I know. He found church as his place to get away from it all, his escape, his solitude.

Halfway through treatments, the thoughts and prayers, strength and determination seemed to be paying off. A party was thrown by the football team. He was going for checkups every three months and things seemed to be going great. Joe was later informed by doctors after finishing Chemotherapy he had reached optimal health, the Lymphoma was gone. He always remained active and upbeat and continued his monthly checkups until finally about a year later the lymph nodes became infected again with Lymphoma. He needed a Biopsy to remove his white blood cells; the plan was an Autologous Bone Marrow Transplant in Boston.

Once again he needed Chemotherapy, except this time to a bigger extent. Four or five days a week for about five or six hours; Joe had to become as close to cancer free as possible to move to Boston for the transplant. After three weeks the Bone Marrow was cleared. He was then put onto a machine where his blood was taken from his veins to collect white blood cells and later on would be given back to him. The next stage was moving onto Boston. Everything was completely sealed off and sterile to avoid any germs. Like he was living in a bubble, he couldn't move, hug family members, or his son. He reassured everyone that he would be alright no matter the thoughts racing through his mind. Tests were continuously run, Chemo was more potent twice a day, and wires were hooked up all around him fighting for his life.

Family eventually was able to visit and movies and games were brought to make everything as normal as possible. Over and over he reassured his son as they sat as close as allowed. A priest came in and said "Happy Birthday" to inject the white blood cells; it symbolized the beginning of his new life. Once the blood count moved to where it had to be, which was up in the millions, and after all the pain, sweat, and tears he was cleared to go home for Easter. When he got home, once again family and friends provided more than enough support. The last step after getting home was going one hundred days alone at home, with testing from the doctors and remaining germ free to be cleared once again of cancer, which is easier said than done.

After those days passed, he did not wait long and he took his son for a celebration to Disneyworld. It was a great time for both of them, not because of all the rides and cartoons, but because they can't get enough of each other. Joe has completed an enormous task and defeated one of the most dangerous diseases known to the world. It shows how strong of a father, son, friend, and person he is. He now goes for check ups every six months instead of three. Thoughts, I'm sure, are always in the back of his mind, but being the strong person he is, he remains positive and is an inspiration. He is an inspiration not only to cancer patients or survivors, but to myself and should be to anyone else who needs someone to look up to for hope.

One other friend of mine is a great woman named Dawn Sinesi. She is the mother of three beautiful daughters and the grandmother of one. Family is very important to her and with these girls in her life it helps to always keep her smiling and to continue fighting. She refuses to give up and is always in a great mood giving the best advice to live by, it's inspiring. She was diagnosed with stage one Breast Cancer in 1996.

After finding a lump in her breast she went to the doctor who informed her that it was nothing major to worry about. When she went in to have a cyst removed from her ovary, the doctor decided to do a needle aspiration on the lump of her breast, which is a biopsy on lumps or bumps to take in tissue to evaluate any problems, such as inflammation or cancer. The doctor then received the results from the needle aspiration and concluded it was nothing serious. After talking with a friend, Dawn came to the conclusion to go see the doctor again who decided to remove the bump; sort of an out of sight, out mind scenario.

Days later she was called and informed that it was cancer, but it was "dangerous and curable." Proceeding with a Lumpectomy, which removes all Lymph Nodes, she began being treated with Radiation only. Her radiation lasted for five and a half weeks, Monday through Friday. The next step was for her to take a pill known as Tamoxifen or a mild form of Chemotherapy for five years.

The pain and aggravation of baring a deadly disease became a part of her new routine and a part of her normal schedule, which built up frustration, and she began to experience hot flashes. Doctors saw it as a sign of depression and she was given Effexor as an anti-depressant. More time passed and after all of her Mammogram tests and ten years of medication went by she was in remission. A weight had been lifted off her shoulders and she could feel herself again. Jogging, getting back into shape, working more and being more active, she felt more alive than she had felt in years.

Being a talented and dedicated woman, Dawn changed professions from working at a salon to becoming a medical assistant. From standing to sitting a lot more on the job she started to experience pain in her lower back and left arm blaming it on career changes. The doctor took an x-ray and spotted a shadow in Dawn's arm and took a Biopsy of the Humerus bone that showed the cancer had spread further, or metastasized over a period of time to the bones. Eleven years later, at age 42, the cancer reappeared as stage four Breast Cancer.

The next step in this ongoing process of battling for life was Chemotherapy. The treatment was much more potent and she had to take a pill everyday. Four years have passed and she has been on five different types of Chemotherapy ranging from oral to having a Portacath, which is a medical apparatus connecting the port to a vein. She became Neutropenic at times, losing her white blood cells, but never losing faith.

She is now off the Chemotheraphy treatment, but is being taken care of hormonally. She receives one injection into her abdomen, two injections into her buttocks, and one into the port in her vein by the drug Zometa, which is used to target the bones as a strengthener. Zometa is a therapy for when the bone metastasizes. The other injections are used to capture the extra estrogen inside her body and close down her ovaries. She is also tested by a Petscan for cancer; her last test was successful on July 1, 2011.

As she continues her fight for life, this woman has battled for over a decade and a half, almost sixteen years! She continues to fight and does nothing but amaze me. She is very wise and would do anything for her children or granddaughter. She is a very nice person who can light up a room and captivate a person's attention; we can all grow from hearing what she has to say. She is positive, wise, sensible, and a great role model. With no regrets in life, on August 3, 2011 she says, "I would accept stage IV cancer again to be where I am today and what I've learned." Her positive attitude, beliefs, strength, ambition, and the affect on her daughters' outlook on life is irreplaceable.

჻ ჻

These three stories, along with Maria Barata, are incredible to hear and they are about people we can look up to. They have battled, or are still battling, so much but have never complained "Why me" once. I'm grateful to have these people in my life because we can learn a lot from hearing them speak or seeing how they go about living life. To persevere you have to want it and have the motivation to follow through with it. Some people have their family or children to worry about and support which can create an extra burden on their mind. It is fascinating to see their success. Once you go through a traumatic health experience I believe people begin to realize and appreciate what they're given in this world and that they need to take advantage of it. Between Robbin Marsland, Joe Acciardo, Dawn Sinesi, Maria Barata and me; we've become even more thankful for everything around us daily and wake up each day knowing life is a privilege.

I'm thankful my family felt it was their top priority to help and watch me succeed. Motivation can be as simple as chasing a championship in sports or as difficult as beating one of the most deadly diseases known to mankind. In my case it was overcoming a traumatic brain injury. You can't just sit around and wallow in your self pity. It's painful and it's a shot to a man's pride because it takes baby steps to overcome this adversity. Recovery doesn't happen overnight, it takes around three years for the brain to be considered fully healed and recovered. Even when I felt like I was ready to jump back into the real world, I wasn't. I was nervous just going out and not being with my brother or people I knew I could trust.

During my recovery process I responded to an article called "Crossroads" found on Boston.com and even Oprah, twice as a matter of fact. I wrote so many verses in a special book my parents bought me for Christmas and wrote to clear my mind some nights. I played Sudoko's over and over again three or four games a day for months and still do a few times a week. I used the brain game book my parents bought me also on Christmas which had a variety of games changing the types up every page from crosswords to word searches to unscrambling words or unscrambling quotes and sayings. I still play different online games called Mahjong or Bookworm where you create words from a big block of letters or in Mahjong you match the blocks up layer-by-layer which helps with my visual and spatial deficits. I've also used a website called "Lumosity" which had tons of games from timed math to creating words beginning with certain letters. Even on my phone I found games, one called unblock me and one I play with friends called words with friends. Anything I can do to help stimulate my mind, I do it. I'm determined and dedicated to come back quicker than anyone ever anticipated, and better than I was before my injury. In my mind, it's mind over matter.

"Only I stand in my way nobody can stop me, I'm not cocky I'm honest, I've gone through hell so I live it up today because tomorrow isn't promised, I'm the farthest from an artist but my words paint pictures, my scriptures speak deep and cut through you like scissors, I'm not bitter I beg to differ pain is temporary, I remain positive an do anything necessary to climb back to the top, cuz you've never reached your peak until you let yourself drop, continue to climb with success on my mind and I play my cards right, because anything worth it is worth the fight in life..."

February 3, 2011

A big part of perseverance is also having hope, something to look forward to or someone to look up to. In my case it is looking up to a state trooper named Brendan Doyle. When I was in the Spaulding Rehabilitation Center and I started to realize a little bit of what I had been through, I thought I was done for. I thought my life as I knew it had just been thrown out of the window of the 8th floor. My friends and my family would come and go and I would sit and stare as time ticked by a minute at a time giving myself no hope. Each hour seemed like a day. I thought this was the rest of my life. I asked myself "Why me?" and "Why won't my parents take me home?" I was begging for answers from anyone who would listen until one day it was all turned around. My parents told me about this man and I pictured in my head Superman. This man became my hero and gave me hope to carry on.

> "*A* desire to be in charge of our own lives, a need
> for control, is born in each of us. It is essential to
> our mental health, and our success, that we take control."
>
> ~Robert Foster Bennett

On June 16, 2007 around two in the morning in Providence, Rhode Island Brendan was struck while off duty only to fall and hit the back of his head on the pavement. He was rushed to Rhode Island hospital and the neurosurgeon opened his skull to remove the pressure on his brain. In the doctor's words he is "miraculous." This man is widely known around here and has the respect of everyone.

Brendan is so mentally strong. He suffered different injuries because of the specific part of the brain that was damaged. After being hospitalized from June 16th to July 9th he was sent to the Spaulding Rehabilitation Center where he experienced speech, occupational, and physical therapy to the maximum extent for three weeks.

As a part of speech therapy he had to learn how to speak again due to slurred speech. Refusing to be defeated he practiced his speech by reading and doing vocal exercises. For occupational therapy he re-learned how to cook, participated in board games, and did other hands on activities with other patients. As far as the physical aspect goes, he was paralyzed on his right side with double vision. He learned how to walk again and did different arm and balancing exercises. He walked straight lines and picked up different articles off the floor while standing on one leg. He was able to walk up and down the stairs and while outside on the Charles River he rowed for a few miles. Eventually, before being cleared to leave, he even ran a half-mile on the treadmill.

After hearing his story from my parents, and considering that he is a state trooper, living just married and working normally, I thought to myself "holy shit!" This man amazes me every time I think about his achievements. It encouraged me and I always think to myself that if he can get his life back then I can do my best to get mine too, its possible.

After just one year, he went back to work as a state trooper. After all the rehabilitation, the training exercises, and the physical and mental qualifications he had to meet, he reached his destination. He re-qualified and for the second time reached his dream of working as a state trooper. He is now not only a state trooper but a detective.

I had the opportunity to meet him four months after my assault and three years after his and we exchanged numbers, I had nothing but smiles and tears of joy. I felt like a little kid, and I went out and told everyone about his story even if they already knew and told everyone that we talk from time to time, bragging proudly. He is my inspiration and also supports traumatic brain injuries. He runs a 5k fundraiser with the state police and people who've suffered traumatic brain injuries. I went on October 23, 2010 to Slater Park, my first one, and I will continue to go to support his cause for as long as he has it. All of the money raised at this event goes to support traumatic brain injuries.

It's amazing to see and learn people's true colors after tragic situations. They either step up with support or fall out of people's lives because they're only worried about themselves, but life goes on. After going through everything and then listening to other stories, I've learned family is the most important thing in life. From the Mercurio's bonding with my family during the roughest of times, or my family simply taking over and getting me the best of help. Also, the stories of Robbin Marsland, Joe Acciardo or Dawn Sinesi fighting for their lives with their children in their corner supporting them no matter what. Once you're affected it seems to change your entire attitude toward everyone else who's trying to battle major circumstances. From Aimee seeing what her mother fought and beat to now finding a group of friends who now support breast cancer; From the outpouring of support and encouragement for Mr. Acciardo to his parents, son, old friends, new friends, and his football team; From the Sinesi daughters supplying so much support and hope for their mother to giving her the will to carry on; From Brendan Doyle supporting traumatic brain injuries and giving back to giving myself hope and support, which showed me how to also give back. People go about their lives not worrying about the smallest things they can do to help when someone has fallen into a bottomless pit. I've learned and became more aware of how easy it is, and how much easier it would be if everyone took a minute to check themselves for an hour, a day, or a dollar.

> *"It's not the size of the dog in the fight, it's the size of the fight in the dog."*
>
> *~Mark Twain*

Charles Darwin, who lived from 1809-1882, put forth the idea of "natural selection" or evolution, which is known or considered when people or animals inherit traits passed down from generations. That eventually led to the phrase "survival of the fittest" which can be seen from two different perspectives. Some refer to it as being the biggest and strongest physically, while others think of it as adapting to an environment and being the most versatile mentally, so it's seen as having a variety of traits. Survival of the fittest to me means all of the above, mind, body, and soul. After this experience I find myself with the entire package and a strong believer in the theory. I'll be the first to say that physically I'm not the biggest or strongest, but my heart is. Mentally I'm never willing to settle, but I am willing to help and to listen. I have no ego, I'm willing to branch out and expand, and I'm willing to hear others and grow from not only my experience, but theirs as well. Just because you're the biggest doesn't mean you'll be the strongest or be able to survive through the roughest of times. You need the entire package, so when one aspect isn't working at its best the two other parts can pickup the slack.

Now, after I gambled with my life on the line I'm the luckiest and richest guy around. I'm rich with knowledge not with dollars. I'm rich in life experience and wisdom beyond my years. Some people may think that's cliché or might say that they would rather take the money and run, but believe me... money can't buy you happiness. Money can't buy you life or the thrill of experience. Money can't make a twenty-two, just turned twenty-three year old party animal into a family oriented person who wants to help change the world for the better. Money can't provide you with the strength to carry on when there's no hope in sight, and all that's surrounding you is failure accompanied by a long, winding trail or obstacles that seem like Mount Everest of a climb. I want to help the people that are affected by the same traumatic experiences I have seen and have been fighting through. When you have more than enough money, that's when you run into greed, envy, and jealousy. When you have more than enough knowledge, you're always sharing it and spreading the wealth with nothing expected in return from the people who appreciate the smaller things.

> "*We must become the change we wish to see in the world.*"
> ~*Mohandas (Mahatma) Gandhi*

Last year before my injury I saw myself just working hard for the rest of my life. I had a job and had just gotten hired for a second job working with my friend Ray at UPS. I planned on having two jobs, an early morning to mid afternoon job and later shifts doing the best I could to get by for the rest of my life. It's funny because after fighting so hard to get back to this life I thought was so illustrious, now I have bigger plans in sight. My number one aspiration, or number one on my bucket list you could call it, is continuing to get healthy quicker than anyone could have ever predicted. Number two is to write a book and open up other people's eyes or give hope. I want to show others who have been put into similar situations that it is not the end of the world. You can grow and become a stronger and better person.

After sixteen months, I find myself back in school when, a few years back, it was a fight to receive my associate's degree. I didn't think I'd ever be back in school with goals of helping people with traumatic brain injuries and becoming an occupational therapist. I want to help with the rehabilitation process and help the patients to believe in themselves. I also want to speak to people because I know what is going on inside of their heads and how to help families. I have lived the experience, so why not make it easier for others to live and fight through it as well?

I've completed a summer course, Psychology with a B- as my final grade. I'm now taking three courses, Intro to Occupational Therapy (OCTA), Medical Terminology, and Oral Communications at both the Providence and Lincoln CCRI campuses. Next semester I have to finish my prerequisites by taking Human Anatomy, Physiology and

Developmental Psychology. After completing those I'm trying to get accepted into a highly respected program on the Newport CCRI campus run by Professor Michael Nardone. They accept just twenty four students a year with the known fact of a 100% pass rate for first time students taking the national examination (NBCOT). Nationally, the graduates have ranked in the top twenty five percentile.

Finally, upon graduation I would like to join the staff at Sargent Rehabilitation. I can offer a different perspective based on my injuries and experiences that would help others better understand their thoughts, feelings and goals. After all of these steps on the ladder to success I hope this book is able to encourage patients, and to be my own occupational therapist. I want to work with patients and to help get them back to their livelihood, capable of doing day to day tasks on their own giving them a great sense of accomplishment. I want to be a representative for people who have suffered traumatic brain injuries which I hope will also boost their confidence.

This whole entire process has been life altering and has opened up my eyes to reality and to how the real world really works, but best of all it leads me down a different path. The road I was on was just like anyone else my age that did not graduate from college or were a little lost from the bigger picture in life. I would work, but hate it, and I would spend more money than I should have, but loved it. Life works in mysterious ways because never in my wildest imagination did I think I would want to complete writing a book and hope and feel it would be able to inspire others, or give them the will and courage to keep on keeping on. When you have to overcome such a monstrous task it is not easy to do on your own and sometimes just by texting my brother late at night because I couldn't sleep I received hope and started to believe again. So by reading this, whether you have had a traumatic brain injury, cancer, or whatever else you think you cannot overcome, maybe you will think twice and others will stand strong by your side, pushing you to your limit to never give up.

I stated before that I wasn't extra close with my brother. He was, however, always there for me through the hardest time of my life. After this struggle filled year I think it opened up more than just my eyes. My brother Nick is quoted as saying "To this day I always think about what would have went differently if I wasn't lazy and drove to the bar to meet up with him or if I just invited him to the party I was going to. I'm very happy to see him making a recovery that not many doctors thought he would make and not at the speed in which he is doing it. I have a whole different outlook on life now and look at my brother as someone to look up to from time to time when he isn't a pain in my ass. The stuff he has to go through and the stuff he has overcome has made him a different person as well. I didn't think he would be doing some of the things he does now like going back to school and writing this book."

With my brothers statement, it just reassures me and makes me more proud of my accomplishments. I've heard people close to me say "what if this" or "what if that," but I've moved on with my life and I hope they don't harbor any guilt because I know who has been in the real fight with me. In my eyes Nick has grown a lot as well from this experience. His newest tattoo dedicated to my experience is from a famous American author and screenwriter, Mario Gianluigi Puzo. "The strength of a family, like the strength of an army, is in it's loyalty to each other." Family comes first, but I like to think everyone who was around me was impacted in a different way. Whether it is direct or indirect, I hope after this on going experience people realize that life is too short. Enjoy the moments you have been given on this Earth to the fullest because you never know when it is your time to go.

"A sound mind in a sound body," is a famous Latin quotation of what the Roman citizens should desire in life, which is good physical and mental health. As a parent what do you always wish for when your child is born? Personally, I always hear, "Boy or girl, I don't care as long as he or she is healthy." Once the child is born though, everyone waits for a bad predicament to come along to fall back into what is really important in life. I stated how money brings greed, envy, and jealousy, and instead of certain desires we need to pursue happiness. Patience is a virtue, a great and rare attribute found in a person, and happiness comes in time. Nothing is handed to you in life, you need to work for it, and when you reach your goal it will be that much sweeter. During my time on this Earth I've decided that no matter what, even when things get rough or look their worst, to enjoy every moment I'm granted.

My parents and I didn't have a clue where to look for help. I looked toward my parents while they looked at each other lost and confused. After looking into different options, they found this group called the Brain Injury Association of Rhode Island. It is a non-profit organization for the survivors who have suffered a traumatic brain injury. Not everyone is as fortunate as I am. This association not only provides support systems to the survivor, but it also helps inform parents and families of the consequences and needs. Members also include health care professionals and physicians. Their mission is to "help prevent and enhance the lives of those affected."

There is a support group located in every state of the country supported by the Brain Injury Association of America. The leading cause is from a fall and a blow to your head. The elderly can also join and receive support from online groups if they are unable to travel by vehicle. If someone is a war veteran they can join the Defense and Veteran Brain Injury Center. I never realized how severe and easy these injuries occur, but a Rhode Island known fact is that a brain injury occurs every hour!

It is a shame how the Providence Police Department reacted that evening I was, assaulted. Assumptions were made by the police that nearly cost me my life. As a first responder, 9-1-1 should have been called by the police. What it looks like and what the actual facts are, are two completely different things. It's all in how you choose to look at it. Proper evaluation of the situation was never completed. Valuable details were never written down regarding the two witnesses on scene, they never even took down their names! I don't know what makes me more upset, them totally screwing up on scene, or how they handled everything afterwards. My brother actually had to go down to the police station and let them know that "his brother was fighting for his life," and they did not even know the severity of the assault. When the police showed up at the hospital, they changed the charges to felony assault, instead of simple assault due to the severity of the crime. In the beginning stages when they seemed to be attempting to settle the case, I walked in the station with my helmet on and took it off for a picture, the detective was completely in shock and had no idea it was that severe. Sitting there with half a skull did prove that As time went by I grew more frustrated because there was never any news. There were never any phones calls from them. They seemed to almost give up in no time as my dad had to stay in contact with them. We supplied them with leads, names and picked out pictures but to no avail. When my Dad would call, all they would tell him was "Sorry no new developments," seeming the least bit interested, after trying to place the name.

In conclusion, I can't thank my parents enough. For all the focus and motivation I've had, they've been just as prepared to battle, and when I wasn't they were already supplied with extra ammunition for the fight. As excited as I was each step of the way in making progress, you could multiply their excitement by ten. Anything they can do, they do. For example, I'm all the way down to one drug, and they're staying on top of me taking my one seizure medication *still*. My dad wakes me up every morning at eight o'clock a.m. before work and my mom takes over at night at eight o'clock p.m. as a reminder. I wouldn't have been able to do this without them. They have given me so much support and encouragement behind the scenes, if only everyone saw and knew how I reacted in the beginning stages and what it was really like at times that I didn't know if it was all worth it. They got me the best rehabilitation services possible, and if they were located in Texas they would have brought me there. I can't thank you enough and I'm proud to say you're my parents. I'm blessed, you continue to support, encourage, and amaze me every day.

Thank you to everyone who has been their in my corner and thanks for all the thoughts and prayers I've received throughout my recovery process. This was by no means a one-man fight and I appreciate everyone from my neurosurgeon to my doctors, physicians, therapists, nurses and aides, my parents, brother, family and friends, thank you for a second chance at life.

"*My heart an soul in my scriptures, I've bared it all to you like a stripper, written down to let you relate, it's love hate because now I'm truly exposed, the only way I **Express** is usually through my clothes, even though we share the same views when it rains outside my thoughts get clouded, who to choose between when success comes along so I always remain grounded, because that's when your circle get's crowded, we're all captive of our own thoughts but the only thing on my mind is to triumph...*"

April 15, 2011

THANK YOU

I want to thank everyone involved in helping me produce this book. A true story on the strength of a family, friends and faith. The struggle and battle to persevere against all odds.

To my parents, for reliving this traumatic experience and for being so clear with their vivid details, descriptions and recollections throughout the entire process.

To Ray Pilkington, for his clear memories of the events that took place.

To my brother, Nick, for his input and point of view.

To Robin Wyllie, for her perspective.

To Robbin Marland, Joseph Acciardo, Dawn Sinesi, Maria Barata, and Brendan Doyle, for their individual stories of their own battles and success.

To Elizabeth Mantelli and Aimee' Marsland for their editing and advice.

Finally, a special thanks to everyone for their thoughts, prayers, support and encouragement from the beginning until the present.

A special dedication for my Grandmother (Nonna), Uncle Eddie, and good friend Marissa Gardner. You all are loved and missed and in my thoughts and prayers.

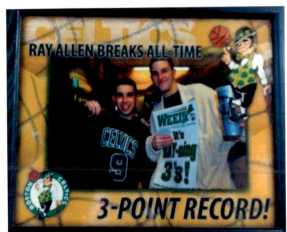